George Clinton

Frontispiece. George Clinton portrait with signature. "Eng[raving] by Williams New York." Collection of The New-York Historical Society. Used with permission.

GEORGE CLINTON

Master Builder of the Empire State

JOHN K. LEE

With a Foreword by JAMES B. BELL

Produced and distributed by

SYRACUSE UNIVERSITY PRESS

For a listing of books published and distributed by Syracuse University Press,
visit our Web site at SyracuseUniversityPress.syr.edu.

ISBN-13: 978–0-8156–8153–3
ISBN-10: 0–8156–8153–4

Produced and distributed by Syracuse University Press
Syracuse, NY 13244–5290

Manufactured in the United States of America

In memory of my wife, Bea

JOHN K. LEE is a graduate of Yale, where he majored in American History.

Most of his business life was with the Center for Marketing Communications in Princeton, where he was its Managing Director when it was merged into the Advertising Research Foundation in New York City.

Later, his work as an independent consultant gave him the opportunity for further historical studies at Princeton University and to write a six-volume series covering the beginnings of the Americas and the growth of the colonies until the eve of their struggle for independence. James B. Bell edited three of these volumes.

JAMES B. BELL, author of this book's foreword, received his doctorate in history from Oxford and has held professorships at universities including Ohio State and Princeton.

His books have dealt mainly with 18th-century English and early American history, his latest being *A War of Religion: Dissenters, Anglicans and the American Revolution*, published by Palgrave Macmillan. During the 1980s, Bell served as Managing Director of The New-York Historical Society. Currently, Dr. Bell is a Fellow at the Rothermere American Institute in Oxford.

Contents

Illustrations

Foreword

James B. Bell

The life and times of New York State's first governor, George Clinton, is little known beyond the band of scholars of the War for Independence and the early period of U.S. history. John K. Lee has admirably redressed this lapse in our historical memory of an eminent state and national leader. It is a study benefiting from wide-range and systematic research, an attractive literary style, and the distinguished assistance of John P. Kaminski, the acknowledged authority on Clinton's life and career and of his continuing study of the American Constitution.

By any measure the life experience of George Clinton was rich, varied, and accomplished. Born on the family farm on July 26, 1739, in Little Britain in Ulster County, today in Orange County, his lifeline stretched across the final decades of the British colonial era through the early years of the New Republic until his death in 1812. He was a witness to and a leading participant in the unfolding civil events in the colonies that began in the 1770s and led to the Declaration of Independence, the Revolutionary War, and the confederation of state governments and of the United States.

The son of Charles Clinton, an Irish immigrant, pioneer settler, and lieutenant colonel of the French and Indian War, George's distinguished personal, professional, and public careers covered more than fifty years. Like many young men of his day Clinton's education was limited to a private tutor. And like those with an adventurous soul young George was lured to sea for a short voyage on an armed vessel. He then became engaged in the military under his older brother James and with his father in the capture by the English of Fort Frontenac and the city of Montreal. Following his military enlistment, Clinton experienced a rapid succession of personal events leading up to his full-time political life. A clerkship of common pleas in Ulster County was arranged in 1759 by a distant relative, colonial Governor George Clinton, and was followed by being admitted to the New York bar in 1764. He was made his county's district attorney the next year. Elected to the colony's Assembly in 1769, Clinton inherited political allies through his marriage to Cornelia Tappan in 1770.

In a period of six years Clinton through his temperament and talent demonstrated a pragmatic turn of mind in the practice of law, his business interests, and colonial affairs. His competence and strength differed notably from other political leaders of his generation. Clinton's intellectual interests did not embrace the historical and philosophical subject that inspired and gripped the attention of John Adams, Thomas Jefferson, James Madison, and Alexander Hamilton. By the late 1760s Clinton had already established himself as a leading opponent of the Crown—partially through his legal maneuvering in support of Alexander McDougall, a merchant who had refused to cooperate with Parliament by refusing to answer if he was a Sons of Liberty member. The publicity emitting from the long-drawn-out jailing and trial was a main factor in furthering the revolutionary movement growing in New York. Parliament's passage of the Sugar Act in 1764 had given Samuel Adams of Massachusetts cause to denounce the imposition of duty on sugar as being "taxation without representation." Like the publicity given to New York's Sons of Liberty, Adam's newspaper writings and essays ushered in a plethora of challenges by radical civil leaders opposed to England's policies. The Stamp Act and Townsend Acts brought on a reaction that led to the Boston Tea Party, and after the battles of Lexington, Concord, and Bunker Hill the rest of the colonies were advocating separation from England.

In this whirlwind of strife Clinton's public life was molded and advanced in the legislature and as a delegate to the Second Continental Congress that met in Philadelphia between May 1775 and July 1776, proceedings that culminated in the Declaration of Independence. As much of the political debate was framed by radical spokesmen and the popular press during the 1770s and afterward, Clinton emerged as a unifying force among a variety of interests, personalities, and factions. His political reputation and accomplishments were shaped by the manner in which he was able to lead and compromise with colleagues in the midst of heated and turbulent legislative proceedings. George Washington, as a delegate from Virginia to the Congress, gained a most favorable impression of Clinton's conduct and bearing during the proceedings and it was there that the two Georges became lifelong friends.

After the Congress appointed Washington as commander-in-chief he requested that Clinton be returned to New York to perform protective services along the Hudson River. Clinton had already done considerable work along the river, and because of this and his leadership qualities he was made a brigadier general in the Continental Line. Both men having been called for military duty prevented their being signers of the Declaration of Independence!

Defensive measures directed by Clinton included the construction of Forts Montgomery and Clinton and other fortifications and the laying of a specially forged chain across the Hudson. Such was the state of preparedness in early July 1776 when the fleet carrying 20,000 troops from England arrived at Staten Island. Under the command of General Sir Henry Clinton, the mission was to undertake a campaign up the Hudson and, by joining forces with England's General John Burgoyne's army on the north, bring about a quick and strategic victory to end the war by separating New England from the other colonies.

That this elegant British plan did not succeed because of a combination of unanticipated events—as related in the text, which includes the destruction of the forts and the heroics of the Clinton brothers—was the single most decisive and fortuitous outcome for the American cause up until that time. Moreover, this series of events provided France with the necessary justification to join the colonies in the war against England.

With the British war plans changing from the Hudson to the southern colonies, conditions were relatively calm in the rest of the state. In June 1777 Clinton was nominated for both governor and lieutenant governor and was elected to both offices thanks to his support from the yeomanry. His election to the governor's office marked a dramatic shift of the traditional dominance in the office by the aristocracy. The man who was his leading civil rival, Philip Schuyler, later became Alexander Hamilton's father-in-law. Clinton then began his first of six successive terms as governor, covering a span of eighteen years.

Early in his governorship Clinton was confronted with another "invasion" of sorts: Loyalists joining up with Iroquois tribes in ravaging the New York and Pennsylvania western frontiers. Plundering and atrocities had reached the point that Clinton's appeal to the Continental Congress resulted in the formation of an army, or about a third of the men in American uniforms at that time. Organized as the Sullivan-Clinton (Gen. James) campaign, its invasion was a complete success in claiming control over all lands south of the St. Lawrence River formerly held by the British. This amounted to about 900,000 square miles, which England was forced to give up in the Treaty of Paris in 1783. This ownership paved the way for America's first major step in western expansion that would lead to the Louisiana Purchase.

After General Lord Cornwallis surrendered the British forces at Yorktown, Virginia, in October 1781, concluding the military campaigns of the Revolutionary War, Clinton's career became focused on state and national affairs in New York. Clinton's continuing leadership helped the state attain the highest economic growth in the nation. His vision foresaw the need for building canals along the Mohawk River, a project that was realized by his nephew, De Witt Clinton.

In addition to serving as governor, Clinton was also much involved as the framer of New York State's constitution. But national affairs shifted his attention when in May 1787 a convention met in Philadelphia to consider revision of the Articles of Confederation. After lengthy debate over several proposals the session instead produced the proposed new federal Constitution that dramatically strengthened the power of the federal government. When it was submitted to the states for ratification in late September 1787, Clinton mobilized his supporters in opposition. Clinton feared that a federal government with the power to regulate commerce as provided in the Constitution could be used to negate New York's commercial hegemony over neighboring states. Because of its fine harbor, New York had natural advantages in trade over other states in the union. In addition, Clinton had built his political machine through the great patronage power provided by the 1777 New York constitution, which he feared might be threatened by a federal charter that could diminish the sovereignty of the states in any way.

The growing division among lawmakers concerning state and federal powers in the Constitution opened up an Anti-Federalist movement by those believing the document favored a too centralized government. However, other than a handful of well-known personages such as Patrick Henry and Richard Henry Lee of Virginia it was George Clinton who became by far the most outspoken critic. Actually, this movement is the story surrounding the Federalist Papers written by Hamilton, James Madison, and John Jay. These papers, some eighty-five of them in the form of essays, were published in the *Daily Advertiser*, New York's leading newspaper, to promote adoption of the Constitution and to rebut the series of letters published in the *New York Journal* that took up the cause of states' rights. These letters were written by George Clinton but signed "Cato." In these letters Clinton made reference to the theory advanced by Montesquieu that republics could only survive in small territories and warned New Yorkers that the Constitution as written would replace a system of sovereign states essential to the preservation of liberty with a consolidated government headed by a chief executive whose powers were too vaguely defined. However, as the exchanges between the Federalist Papers and Clinton's letters played out, it was becoming obvious that the great majority of the states favored adoption of the Constitution. Under the circumstances Clinton realized he needed to do all he could to have his political thinking adopted. First of all was the need for a Bill of Rights, which he discussed with Jefferson and in turn could have resulted in Madison writing it. Then, by holding out on ratification Clinton could exert all the pressure he could to advance states' rights.

Clinton's opposition to ratification cost him much political support in New York. In the 1789 gubernatorial contest he was only able to secure a slim majority for his reelection. Three years later it took the partisan machinations of the state-elected canvassers, who threw out the ballots of three counties that had provided the margin of victory for his opponent, to keep Clinton in office. Nonetheless, a Federalist majority in the Assembly curtailed much of the governor's power. In 1795, facing certain defeat at the hands of the New York electorate, Clinton decided to retire from the post.

But earlier events were destined to chart a new phase in Clinton's public career. During the summer of 1791 Thomas Jefferson and James Madison made a trip through New York State, a journey that historians have reasoned was to seek political allies by rekindling an old issue of states' rights that had not died away. Although Madison had been at the constitutional convention as a passionate advocate of federal power, he later modified his position by sharing with Jefferson the belief the federal government was becoming harmful under the control of Alexander Hamilton. However, inconsistently, he further agreed that because opposition in the states as in Virginia was the most available antidote, the new Republican political faction should advocate states' rights. Why then should there not be a coalition between Virginia and the powerful group in New York that was ambivalent about the whole conception of a federal government?

It is possible that Jefferson and Madison began at this time to build their political alliance with Clinton, who with Robert Livingston and Aaron Burr helped Jefferson to organize the Democratic-Republican faction late in Washington's first administration. The new political group then developed from the cleavage of the Federalist and Anti-Federalists groups. The election of Jefferson as president in 1800 brought the party into power and in control of both houses of Congress through the administrations of Jefferson, Madison, and Monroe (1801–25). Clinton served as vice president during Jefferson's second administration and during Madison's first administration until his death in Washington on April 20, 1812.

In retrospection of Clinton's involvement on the national scene, he emerged alongside all of the political leaders of that time. Despite his differences with Hamilton and other Federalists, Clinton was recognized by political aspirants of both parties as being in contention as Washington's first vice president. But it was his twenty-one years as governor of New York State that endeared Clinton to his constituents. He earned a great deal of gratitude to those who witnessed his service through the Revolution, including putting an end to uprisings on the frontier. Throughout his governorships his management skills in framing the state's constitution and in maintaining state finances under tight control placed New York State in the forefront of other states.

George Clinton was much more than "founder" or "father" of New York State. He was, as John Lee adroitly describes him, *Master Builder of the Empire State.* Inevitably, as a historian, several questions emerge regarding George Clinton's long public career. What would have been the course of civil affairs if he had not repeatedly championed in the New York Assembly the interests of small farmers and merchants over the traditionally dominant landowners and commercial leaders of

the region? What if he had not strategically
executed the defensive military measures at
the present-day site of the West Point Military
Academy in the Hudson River Valley? Through
his highly recognized stature gained as a wartime governor, what would have happened
if he had not gained congressional approval
for a special army that resulted in expelling
the British from all their land below Canada?
What if he had not entered the heated constitutional controversy over states' rights? There
are no answers to these questions. If he had
not been on the public stage perhaps another
or a handful of leaders would have stepped
forward and filled the gap in one or more of
these matters. But we do know that New York's
history and the chronicle of the United States
would have most likely taken a different course
without his leadership.

Preface

The winning of the American Revolution and the founding of the United States produced more recognized military-government personages here and abroad than any other similar grouping in world history except for those in World War II.

In addition to the well-known names of George Washington, John Adams, Thomas Jefferson, Alexander Hamilton, and Benjamin Franklin are others such as Samuel Adams, Paul Revere, Ethan Allen, and Patrick Henry whose names are recognized by many Americans.

And then there are others who are recognized not so much for their exploits or accomplishments as for their other involvements. Such is the case with Benedict Arnold, who led his army through the wilderness of Maine to make an ill-fated assault on Quebec City on New Year's Eve, 1775. Arnold further distinguished himself in engagements against Gen. Burgoyne and his strategic victories in the battles of Saratoga, which influenced France to aid the American cause. After Washington placed him in command of the Philadelphia sector, Arnold through his second wife's Loyalist influence became involved with the British cause and now is generally known as a traitor to his country.

Aaron Burr is another example of one who is remembered not for his military and government service but for his duel that resulted in Hamilton's death. Although not a military hero, Burr did serve under Arnold during the Quebec campaign before joining Washington's staff. After resigning from service due to ill health, Burr was elected to the New York legislature and progressed through state politics to become its U.S. senator and then vice president under Jefferson before the duel.

Another name quite well known is John Hancock, the first to sign the Declaration of Independence. His prolonged signature, much larger than any of the others, led to the frequently used expression of "your John Hancock goes here" when explaining where to sign a document. Only historical "buffs" might know that Hancock and Samuel Adams were the recognized patriot leaders after the Boston Massacre of 1770. Following his presidency of the Continental Congress from 1775 to 1777, Hancock was elected governor of Massachusetts and reelected eight more times.

In contrast to those named above who will be remembered for the reasons cited, George Clinton, New York State's first governor, who served eight terms and was twice vice president of the United States, is all but forgotten. The most likely reason for such lack of recognition is the same for most former vice presidents and governors who are soon forgotten after several successors. With respect to Clinton, there were so many notable personages at that time that his participation in national affairs was on a secondary and, therefore, on a seemingly nonmemorable level. For example, he was well known among his peers for sharing the same political philosophy with Jefferson and at the same time for having to deal with the ultra-conservative Hamilton, a fellow New Yorker. Also, as head of the Senate while he was vice president, Clinton was involved in a number of important policy decisions. One noteworthy example was his casting of the deciding vote against rechartering the Bank of the United States, which had been Hamilton's "regulator" of the Federalist system.

The same reasons for Clinton's lack of recognition apply to his military life. Although he was involved throughout the entire Revolution, his contributions were more on a local level as compared with those who participated in other better known strategic battles whose military leaders are remembered in books and national and state park exhibits.

Although the exploits of many of the Revolutionary War heroes and founding fathers continue to be recounted, it was not until 1938 that E. Wilder Spaulding was prompted to write *His Excellency George Clinton, Critic of the Constitution* by recognizing that Clinton was the most important individual in American history who had not had a biography written about him. Nothing further of particular note was written biographically about Clinton until 1993 with the publication of John P. Kaminski's *George Clinton: Yeoman Politician of the New Republic*.[1] This 294-page volume was sponsored by the New York State Commission on the Bicentennial of the United States Constitution and commemorated the 250th anniversary of Clinton's birth.

The biographies by Kaminski and Spaulding inspired me to continue presenting Clinton's accomplishments with hopes that his contributions are appreciated by the widest readership possible. In this endeavor I have tried to extract for the reader the most salient and interesting material from their writings.

Most significant are their narrations of Clinton's contributions in winning the Revolution. As commander of New York's militia and as a Continental general, Clinton was involved in most of New York's military operations in the state, where nearly one-third of all Revolutionary War engagements took place.

Another valuable contribution dealt with by his biographers concerns the part Clinton and New York legislators played in the state versus federal debates during the adoption of the U.S. Constitution and the effects they had in giving birth to political parties.[2]

Another area of particular emphasis brought out in this condensed biography is the military, social, and business relationship between Clinton and Washington, the closest of friends—another subject that has been passed over by many historians concerned with the Revolutionary period. This friendship had its beginning when Clinton was serving as New York's representative to the Second Continental Congress in Philadelphia in 1775. Later, in October 1777, when Clinton was serving as governor, Washington persuaded Clinton to return to New York, where he was needed most to help prevent Burgoyne's army in the north from joining up with Sir Henry Clinton's army after its plan to move from Nova Scotia to the New York City area.

Both the Americans and British realized that control of the Hudson River would be critical in the eventual outcome of the war. In *Chaining the Hudson*, Lincoln Diamant quotes Washington's own assessment of the situation when writing to one of his generals:

> The importance of the Hudson River in the present Contest, and the necessity of defending it, are Subjects which have been so frequently and fully discussed, and are so well understood, that it is unnecessary to enlarge upon them. These Facts at once

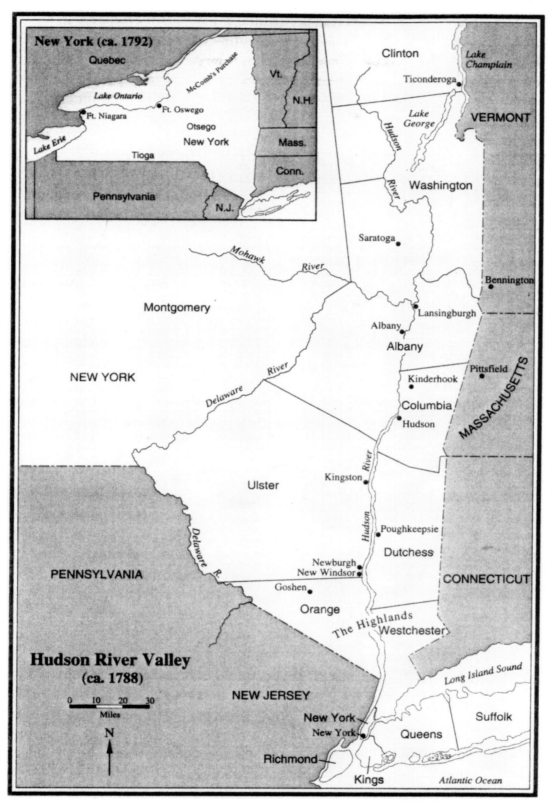

1. Map of the Hudson River Valley, ca. 1788. Reproduced from Kaminski, *George Clinton: Yeoman Politician of the New Republic*. Used with permission.

Sir Henry Clinton

Knight of the Bath & Commander in Chief in America

2. Sir Henry Clinton. Collection of The New-York Historical Society. Used with permission.

appear, when it is considered that the river runs through a whole State; that it is the only passage by which the enemy from New York, or any Part of our Coast, can ever hope to cooperate with an army from Canada; that the possession of it is indispensably essential to preserve the Communications between the Eastern, Middle and Southern States.[3]

Before moving his army from Boston to New York, Washington and Clinton had been in close communication with each other on military matters concerning the Hudson. Because of this association, both men got to know their similarities in background, activities, and interests, all of which developed into a lifelong friendship. Washington and Clinton were men of the soil. Although of aristocratic heritage, both were farmers and both learned to be surveyors. Their travels during the French and Indian War and thereafter gave them an awareness of an expanding frontier and the possibilities it could offer, such as envisioning the building of canals along key river ways. From the outset of their business lives this appreciation of land became their continuing aspiration to acquire. In this regard, Joseph J. Ellis, in *His Excellency George Washington*, while discussing Washington's feelings concerning ownership of land, believed Washington considered land the best means of financial security.[4]

And so it was also with Clinton, who purchased acreage to the extent of it becoming his largest asset. Clinton and Washington together purchased a large tract of land after the war while they were traveling together for three weeks exploring western New York.

AS DISCUSSED EARLIER, the name George Clinton is hardly recognized even among New Yorkers. Added to the reasons stated is the confusion of his name with Sir Henry Clinton, his distant cousin, who is one of the most recognized Revolutionary War personages, having been Britain's commander-in-chief of American military operations after 1778; most of his activities were in the New York colony. It is ironic that George Clinton's chief adversary was Sir Henry, the son of New York's provincial governor George Clinton (1743–53), who had befriended our George Clinton when he was a boy.

Sir Henry has been rated as possibly the best of the British commanders. He began his military training in England at the age of nineteen and served in three campaigns of the Seven Years' War. After becoming a general at the age of thirty-four he went to America in 1775 as second-in-command to Gen. Sir William Howe and fought with distinction at Bunker Hill and Long Island.

Sir Henry was well acquainted with lower New York environs, having lived in the city where his father served as governor of the Province for ten years. During that time Sir Henry also had the opportunity to travel in the Hudson valley, where he later inherited a 4,000-acre tract of land in Ulster County. After the expiration of his father's term as governor the family returned to England.

Acknowledgments

A considerable debt is owed to John P. Kaminski, Ph.D., for the information I culled from his detailed biography of Clinton and for all he did in his critique of my manuscript.

I am fortunate to have James B. Bell, a recognized scholar and author of the American colonial period, to undertake this book's foreword. His overview provides a valuable historical contribution in documenting Clinton as being the leading Anti-Federalist and the foremost champion of states' rights.

I give heartfelt thanks to the staff of Syracuse University Press for assistance from the idea stage all the way to making this book the finest possible. This includes the thorough editing of my manuscript and the creative input of all phases of the production process.

Borrowing privileges at Princeton University Library and the Princeton Public Library, which searched and obtained loans from outside libraries, were indispensable in my work.

The staff of The New-York Historical Society's Department of Rights and Reproduction provided an integral service in assisting with the selection of illustrations as credited. By the same token, those at the Prints and Photograph Division at the Library of Congress made available the most suitable picture of Washington and Clinton leading the triumphal procession. The New York City Library is recognized for furnishing the print of *The Death of Hamilton*.

A special note of thanks goes to the Special Projects Manager at New York City Hall for providing the color photograph of John Trumbull's painting of George Clinton as used on the cover of this book.

Carrie Palmer and Sally Robinson were most helpful in analyzing the text to ensure reader comprehension at the general level.

Throughout the development of the manuscript Sherrill Byrnes's aid was invaluable in computer copy preparation and its transmission to Syracuse University Press. Such is the case for the Department of Information Services at the Hun School of Princeton, which provided its technical facilities in transmitting images of the book's illustrations.

I want to recognize Charles B. Straut (Barney) for introducing me a number of years ago to the study of anthropology, which became the basis for my historical writings.

George Clinton

I

Leading Up to a Political Life

THE CLINTON FAMILY

Like George Washington, George Clinton was descended from "landed" forefathers; his ancestry goes back to Lord Henry Percy, known as the legendary Hotspur. More immediately, Kaminski's research recorded that George's grandfather James Clinton was rewarded with an estate in county Langford in central Ireland for his services in supporting William of Orange during the English revolution.[1]

It was at Glengary, as the estate was known, that George's father Charles was born. Life on the estate was short-lived because of the discrimination against Presbyterians (being the Clinton affiliation) with the return of England's Anglican-based government. Consequently, the Clintons and some 400 others sailed for America in May 1729. George's parents survived the voyage but two of their children succumbed to a measles epidemic that killed more than 90 others. After landing at Cape Cod, the Clintons moved on to Little Britain in New York's Ulster County, about twenty miles from New Windsor, on the Hudson River, which would become George's home upon his marriage in 1770.

A FORTUITOUS BEGINNING FOR YOUNG GEORGE

Because farming on the New Britain homestead did not provide sufficient income, George's father learned to be a surveyor. His capabilities in this work resulted in his being hired by the province's surveyor general to survey land on the developing frontier. This work in turn was brought to the attention of a distant relative, New York's provincial governor George Clinton, who in 1748 offered Charles a selection of positions in government service. Although Charles declined in favor of continuing with his surveying work, this relationship led to the favorable impression of the governor for his namesake, Charles's nine-year-old son. This liking was so favorable that the governor arranged for George to become clerk of the court of common pleas of Ulster County upon the death of the incumbent.

Because of this sudden change of events combined with there being no schools in the nearby area, Kaminski reported, Charles employed a private tutor to start early on to prepare George for the clerkship. It was during this schooling period that George learned and assisted his father in the surveying trade.[2]

George turned eighteen when the French and Indian War was under way and enlisted as a steward's mate on the *Defiance*, a privateer with 16 guns and a crew of 140. During

3. Birthplace of George Clinton, Little Britain, New York. From *Olde Ulster*, March 1909, 79.

the ten-month voyage in the Caribbean the *Defiance* was involved in the capture of several ships, and George probably received some of the prize money.[3]

After returning from his enlistment George learned that his father had been made a lieutenant colonel in the militia and his older brother James a captain. Following their return from the campaign against Fort Frontenac, George at the age of twenty (in 1759) took on the clerkship he had inherited. This duty was soon interrupted when he enlisted as a subaltern in his brother James's company in the successful campaign of wresting Montreal from the French.

Once again conditions were such that George could resume his clerkship. This time he recognized the advantages of furthering his knowledge of the law and decided to become a lawyer. One may assume that George had the proper introduction to be taken on to study law under William Smith in New York City, who was widely recognized for his proficiency as an attorney. Smith was also known for his questioning of Parliament's authority, and his definite radical leanings had a great influence on his young student.

Clinton was admitted to the New York bar in September 1764 and was awarded the position of surrogate for Ulster County. In addition to his law practice he was heavily involved in survey work that would continue on for some time to supplement his income. His experience included surveying the boundary between New York and New Jersey in the summer before his bar acceptance.

WITNESSING A GROWING RESISTANCE AGAINST THE CROWN

By the time Clinton had been admitted to the bar in 1764, an alarming unrest had spread throughout the colonies in opposition to taxes imposed by Parliament. First of these was the Sugar Act of 1764, and then the Stamp Act was enacted to tax such things as legal documents and newspapers. This was followed by the Townsend Acts, which levied taxes on the importation of glass, paper, tea, and other items. These taxes, taking place in the mid 1760s, met with such opposition that Parliament repealed all except for the one on tea.

Revocation of these taxes, however, did not quell opposition to such measures by a growing population wanting to go about their independent ways. Some of these sentiments had grown to the extent of advocating the severance of governmental ties with England. Most active in this pursuit were the Sons of Liberty. This organization founded by Samuel Adams of Boston advocated military action if necessary to attain independence. Expansion of Sons of Liberty membership into other colonies led George III in 1768 to order his royal governors to dissolve any of their legislative assemblies favoring such an organization.

A UNIQUE POLITICAL SITUATION IN NEW YORK

Following up on the king's order, New York's colonial governor, Henry Moore, found it expedient to dissolve the Assembly and to hold elections in 1768 and again in January 1769.

Before these elections took place, the Livingston party had controlled the Assembly for the previous three years. This party was represented mostly by those living in the Hudson River valley, which included early Dutch manor lands occupied by families such as the Rensselaers, Schuylers, Tappans, and Van Courtlands. While these families tried to continue their independent ways enjoyed before England's takeover, they at the same time found it practical to accept Parliament's mandates as best their legislators could manage. Conflicting with this situation, however, was considerable more anti-Parliament conduct by Ulster County and those west of the Hudson. These counties bordering New York's frontier had been settled by farmers, trades people, artisans—"yeomen," as Kaminski characterized them in his George Clinton biography.[4] Many of these, such as the Clintons, were Presbyterians who had brought with them from England their differences with the Anglicans. Accordingly, their representatives were more outspoken.

The opposition party was the Delancey party, a name derived from a prosperous mercantile family in Manhattan, where others were engaged in trading activities with England. The city and adjacent counties where the Delanceys held sway were the stronghold of the Tories, the name given to those loyal to the Crown. The area was also populated by a large number of Church of England members, many of which became avowed Loyalists when war broke out. This total constituency was referred to as the "Court" party for its accommodation in dealing with Parliament.

Significant changes in conditions affecting both of these political parties had been taking place in the few years before the two elections. The rescinding of the Townsend Acts, in particular, provided substantial monetary rewards for the mercantile interests in New York City. This prosperity was shared by a rapidly growing population with the most natural and accessible seaport in the 13 colonies. By the mid-1760s the city had perhaps 20,000 inhabitants and had surpassed Boston. Meanwhile, the Hudson River valley had not experienced similar growth.

It was no wonder, then, that when the votes were tallied after the January 1769 election, the Livingstons were outnumbered 18 to 8.

THE YOUNG LAWYER BECOMES IMMERSED IN POLITICS

Because of his favorable record as a surrogate and the growing recognition of the family name, the Ulster County freeholders elected Clinton two times to the Assembly. His being elected would soon prove to be the turning point from his allegiance to the Crown to becoming a recognized anti-Parliament figure.

This transformation came about through his becoming involved in the McDougall affair. Circumstances precipitating this case began with the Delancey-controlled Assembly authorizing funds for the support of English troops in New York. Despite Clinton having accepted the clerkship from the former colonial governor and being still loyal to England, he found it his duty in representing his constituency to vote against such support.

Several days after the support vote a hand bill denouncing the authorization had been distributed in various parts of the city. When the Assembly discovered that the author of the bill was a prominent merchant, Alexander McDougall, who was also suspected as being a Sons of Liberty member, he was arrested on charges of fomenting seditious action and placed in jail.

McDougall's jailing brought about so much indignation by anti-Parliament groups that he was released several months later. Still under indictment, he was brought before the Assembly for further questioning. It was when McDougall was asked if he was a Sons of Liberty member that Clinton intervened, pointing out that the case was pending in the civil courts. Despite this argument and after refusing to cooperate with the Assembly, McDougall was returned to jail. Clinton was among five voting against this action. McDougall was eventually released from jail for lack of evidence upon the death of the Assembly's chief witness.

Not only did Clinton gain an appreciated recognition for his efforts among the growing number of patriots, but as observed by Kaminski, the affair marked a turning point in the revolutionary movement in New York.[5]

POLITICAL ALLIES INHERITED THROUGH MARRIAGE

While practicing law when the Assembly was not in session, Clinton's work frequently took him to Kingston, county seat for Ulster County, providing the opportunity for his courting of Cornelia Tappan, the daughter of the town's eminent burgher. One of the "manor" families, the Tappans were related to the Wynkoops, Livingstons, and other prominent and wealthy Dutch families who were fervent opponents of the English crown.

In 1770, when they were married, Cornelia was about twenty-six. She had a health deficiency that curtailed their social life. Despite her health she was to bear six children over a 13-year span. According to Spaulding in his biography of George Clinton, the marriage was a devoted one; despite Clinton's heavy government work schedule "his family always remained his first and chief interest."[6]

After the marriage the Clintons moved to a farm overlooking the Hudson.[7] Later that year their first daughter, Catharine, was born. She would later on marry a Van Courtland. Then, nearly four years later, Cornelia was born. She would go on to marry the French minister known as "Citizen" Genêt, who is discussed in chapter 6.

It was not until after the war and their move to Dutchess County that the Clinton's only son, George Washington, was born in 1781. He would become, as Spaulding put it, a "ne'er-do-well" who died at the age of thirty-two.[8] One of the next three sisters was Martha Washington, who died in her twelfth year.

Among Clinton's family relations were the De Witts, another prominent Dutch family. George Clinton's older brother James, when a brigadier general in the militia, married Mary De Witt in 1765. Their son became governor of New York, a U.S. senator, and chief sponsor of the project to build the Erie Canal.

NEW YORK'S RELATIONS WITH ENGLAND BEGIN FALLING APART

During the three years after Clinton's marriage, nothing of substantial importance transpired in the Assembly's deliberations. Then, in 1773 the Boston Tea Party and Parliament's closing of its seaport to all commerce triggered New York merchants from also refusing to accept shipments of tea. When Parliament enforced similar retaliation, the Assembly proposed the formation of a continental congress—which Massachusetts had previously requested—for the purpose of bringing all colonial grievances directly before the Crown.

Such proposals resulted in the First Continental Congress, which met at Philadelphia in the fall of 1774. Represented by delegates from all of the colonies except Georgia, agreement was reached to cease importations and exportations to Britain until rights for Americans were observed, protesting to the Crown that its government had violated colonial charter rights that gave protection for the natural rights of mankind being the same as for those residing in England.

When this ultimate proposal was considered by New York's Assembly, the conservative Tory majority, fearing such conditions as too drastic, mustered a vote of 11 to 10 against adoption. In his discussion of the debate on the issues, Spaulding quotes a historian of the time of Clinton as having declared "that while he could not draw his sword against the King in any but an urgent cause, the time was drawing near when the colonies must arm—and the sooner men realized it the better."[9]

After the Assembly refused to send delegates to the Second Continental Congress, "radical" members asked their county committeemen to send representatives to a convention where delegates to the Congress could be selected. George Clinton was among the twelve chosen, seven of whom had served on the Congress of 1774.

CLINTON LEAVES CONGRESS FOR DUTIES IN NEW YORK

News of the Battle of Lexington in April 1775 led to the dissolution of New York's Crown government despite the majority of New Yorkers, consisting of many Loyalist sympathizers, still not wanting to sever ties with England. Under these circumstances New York "patriots" (the name then becoming in use throughout the colonies) formed a Committee of One Hundred,

which governed New York until the Second Continental Congress met in May 1775.

For the period before attending the Congress in Philadelphia, Clinton was mostly engaged with military preparations in the event of war. In advancing this work he and the other New York delegates persuaded the Congress that the installation of artillery placements on the highlands of the Hudson and along the river to prevent passage of enemy vessels was a necessary priority.

Such precautions were none too soon because later that month New York became engaged in hostilities after Ethan Allen's capture of Ft. Ticonderoga. When the Battle of Bunker Hill took place in mid-June, the Congress responded quickly in naming Washington as the commander-in-chief. Congress also placed Washington in charge of American forces in New York, where control of the Hudson River was necessary to contain the British troops located in Canada and Massachusetts.

Under Washington's directives little time was lost in organizing an army for an assault on British forces in Canada. In the early fall, four New York regiments and two from Connecticut were organized under General Richard Montgomery, of the Livingston family. The Third New York Regiment was under the command of Col. James Clinton, George's older brother.

After this army had won a decisive victory in driving Britain's main Canadian army out of Montreal to Quebec City, the army suffered an ill-fated loss in a surprise attack on the city on New Year's Eve (December 31, 1775), during which Montgomery was killed.

George Clinton was still serving as a congressional delegate while these events were taking place. However, when he was on leave he was in close touch with Washington concerning military matters in New York. Washington recommended Clinton's full-time service in

4. George Clinton in military uniform. Collection of The New-York Historical Society. Used with permission.

New York, and he was named a brigadier general in the Continental Line and by the New York Provisional Congress as the brigadier general in command of the Ulster-Orange County militia.

Spaulding points out that although Clinton had been present in sessions when the Declaration of Independence was being drafted, he was not present in Philadelphia to sign this historic document because of his military service in New York.[10]

2

Clinton as Wartime Governor

THE REVOLUTION TRANSFERS TO NEW YORK CITY

Following the Battle of Bunker Hill, Britain's army, which had suffered more than 1,100 casualties,[1] chose to remain in the Boston area where, from its protective location, the next move could be worked out. Washington also decided to station his army in the Boston area during the fall of 1775, hoping to force the British to attack or retreat before spring, when reinforcements would arrive from England. After the British retreated to Nova Scotia, Washington moved his army to New York City, where he had predicted the British, under commander-in-chief Gen. Sir William Howe, would amass an enlarged army to begin an invasion.

Once the move of his army to lower Manhattan had been made, Washington was faced with the problem of how to deploy his forces to defend the city. His second-in-command Gen. Charles Lee, a recognized authority on defense measures, had convinced Washington that the island could not itself be defended because of Britain's naval superiority, so Lee advocated the fortification of Brooklyn Heights directly across the East River as the best plan for staving off an invasion of the city. Accordingly, Washington began ordering the construction of a series of forts and earthworks in the Brooklyn area.

INVASION THREAT MAKES CLINTON A MILITARY LEADER

Washington's prediction of Britain's plan of invading New York came true on July 11, 1776, when Gen. William Howe's brother, Adm. Sir Richard Howe, landed a flotilla of 20,000 troops on Staten Island. Upon learning of an impending invasion George Clinton summoned his three regiments and dispatched them to Fort Constitution, which was on the Hudson River across from West Point, and to Fort Montgomery, which was across the river from Bear Mountain and was where he established his headquarters. Clinton was immediately involved in preparations for laying a chain across the river to prevent passage of British ships.

Clinton was also involved with the construction of underwater obstacles to impede passage of enemy ships. These included the strategic placement of logs and mounds of rocks to help protect fortifications on or near the river.

While this work was going on, New York's Provincial Congress added the militia of Dutchess and Westchester counties to Clinton's brigade, making a total of five regiments under his command. Also, Washington was requested to appoint an officer to have overall command of the security of the lower Hudson. In appointing Clinton to this responsibility, Washington wrote to the Congress that "General Clinton on all Accounts appears to me the most suitable Person and . . . His acquaintance with the Country, abilities and zeal for the Cause are the Motives that induced me to make choice of him."[2]

Soon after, on August 8, Clinton was ordered to leave 200 men at Bear Mountain and to transfer the remainder of his troops to Fort Kingsbridge just across the Harlem River from the north end of Manhattan. This fort had been newly built as part of a line of defense against any further British invasion. As soon as this transfer was completed, Clinton and another New York brigade were placed under the command of Gen. William Heath, a newly commissioned officer. Hardly had these orders been effected than news was received of the disastrous defeat of American forces in the Battle of Brooklyn, often referred to as the Battle of Long Island.

THE BATTLE OF BROOKLYN AND A TRUCE OFFER

In preparation for the field of battle, Washington had placed Gen. Nathanael Greene in command both for his military abilities and his knowledge of the area's terrain. Unfortunately, Greene became seriously ill less than a week before the battle and was replaced by two generals not familiar with the terrain. Consequently, a critical area was left undefended.

Between August 22 and 25, Gen. Howe had moved his enlarged army of 32,000 troops near the tip end of Long Island. On the following night under the cover of darkness his army outflanked the American main line of defense deployed on the ridge overlooking Brooklyn. In the ensuing battle later that day about 300 Americans were killed while 1,100 others were wounded or captured. The remaining American troops managed to retreat to their Brooklyn fortifications.

Having been forced to the precarious position of being surrounded, Washington feared

a momentary overrun of his army by Gen. Howe's regrouped forces. Fortunately, that afternoon a northeaster storm pelted the area, preventing battle and also keeping the British fleet out of the East River. When Howe's assault did not take place the following day, Washington, in demonstrating his indomitable fortitude and uncanny ingenuity, ordered his officers in Manhattan to corral all available boats and crafts to make the two-mile round trip in transporting his entire army of 9,500 with their supplies across the East River—all without detection by the enemy.

Despite Washington's escape, Gen. Howe, believing that with his vastly larger army he had the Americans on the run, thought this would be the ideal time to seek a truce without further loss of life. Accordingly he arranged a peace mission with representatives of the Continental Congress, but it failed after several weeks of negotiations.

During this interval Clinton, on orders received by Gen. Heath from Washington, was dispatching reconnaissance parties to Long Island to help keep track of British troop movements. Clinton himself was to have performed one of these missions, but it was called off when enemy ships were sighted.

Also during this interval was America's submarine attack on a British warship. Lincoln Diamant, in his *Chaining the Hudson*, describes the maneuvers of the Turtle on the night of September 6, 1776, when "the world had its first taste of submarine warfare."[3] The submarine, as illustrated, was invented by David Bushnell, a thirty-five-year old student at Yale, where he constructed the Turtle. The submarine's hand-driven propeller could move the craft about three miles per hour. Another propeller was for ascending to the top of the water to obtain a fresh supply of air. Another Bushnell invention was what he called a "torpedo," a container filled with powder and a timing device. When the submarine hooked a

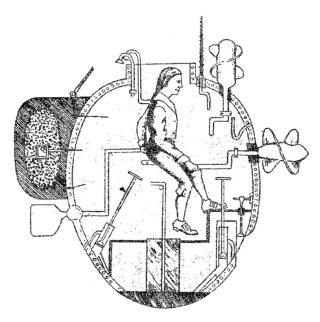

5. Early 19th-century depiction of Bushnell's *American Turtle*. From Diamant, *Chaining the Hudson*. Used with permission.

torpedo to the bottom of a ship being attacked, a timer allowed the submarine to move a distance free of the explosion.

Having learned of the successful trials of the Turtle, Dr. Benjamin Gale, a recognized scientist, described the pertinent details of the submarine in a letter of August 7, 1775, to Benjamin Franklin. Franklin was so interested that he wrote to a New York congressman for additional details. However, further experimentation was postponed until spring, when the British were moving troops into the New York harbor. Then, Connecticut's governor succeeded in getting Washington's approval to have the Turtle shipped to New York's East River in early August.

BUSHNELL'S BROTHER, experienced in navigating the Turtle, was to have manned it on its first attempted attack but illness prevented it. In his stead Ezra Lee, a naval volunteer, was trained in maneuvering for about ten days, during which time Brooklyn had been captured and

Washington had escaped to New York. Then, on the night of September 6, the Turtle was towed by a whale boat to the stern of Adm. Howe's flagship, HMS *Eagle*, where in the words of Lee:

> I could see the men on the deck & hear them talk—I then shut down the doors, sunk down, and came under the bottom of the ship—Up with the screw against the bottom, but found it would not enter. I pulled along to try another place, but deviated a little one side, and immediately rose with great velocity and come above the surface 2 or 3 feet between the ship and daylight—then sunk again like a porpoise.[4]

An hour later after returning to his port. Lee reported that the torpedo suddenly "went off with a tremendous explosion, throwing up large bodies of water to an immense height."

About a week later the Turtle was towed up the Hudson just below Fort Washington. This time the target was an enemy frigate, which spotted the Turtle. Lee's mission was aborted and the submarine was not employed again.

THE RETREAT AFTER THE EVACUATION OF NEW YORK CITY

The weeks consumed with the truce negotiations were a windfall in providing time to decide on whether to evacuate all of Manhattan and move to a more defensive location. Congress placed the decision with Washington, who on September 12 convened a council of war composed of 13 generals, including Clinton and Heath. Fearing that the British would surround the city and cut off communications, the majority, including Washington, opted for a withdrawal. Clinton and Heath, however, believed in making a stand to avoid being pursued elsewhere.[5] For Clinton to have had the courage to speak his mind in this situation demonstrates the rapport and respect that had developed between Clinton and Washington in such a short time.

On September 14, soon after the truce negotiations were called off, Washington began moving his army to Harlem Heights on the west side of the Hudson River and some 20 blocks south of the present George Washington Bridge. The next day Howe's army began its occupation of the city and continued the following day in pursuit of the Americans.

Meanwhile, Clinton led a contingent of Heath's command from Kingsbridge to supplement the main army at the Heights. Clinton got his first experience in battle when several days later Howe attacked the center of Washington's line. In this Battle of Harlem Heights the British were repulsed. Spaulding quotes Clinton writing to the Congress that the battle "has animated our Troops & gave them new spirits & erased every bad impression the Retreat from Long Island &c. had left on their minds."[6]

In the lull following the battle, Washington made an attempt to prevent supplies and equipment left behind by his army on Long Island from falling into British hands. As part of this plan Clinton was ordered to form an expedition leaving from New Haven, Connecticut. However, with Howe on the move again Clinton had to return to Kingsbridge, where his command was to join the main army that was moving to White Plains, where Howe had moved to force Washington into battle.

In the ensuing battle on October 28 the British had 250 casualties, twice those of the Americans. Although Howe's army was victorious, David McCullough concluded that the victory was of no significance.[7] The results of the battle could, however, have played a part in causing Howe to change his strategy in pursuit of Washington.

Howe's new plan was to move his army southwest and capture Fort Washington on the Hudson off present-day George Washington Bridge. Success of this operation would be the first step in control of the river or in capturing Fort Lee across the river. The latter objective was to prevent Washington's army from crossing the Hudson, where he could obtain additional troops in New Jersey.

Surmising these plans from whatever intelligence he had, Washington lost no time in dividing his army to escape Howe's pursuit and to maintain control of the Hudson. Before Howe could make his move to the river, Washington placed troops under Gen. Heath to guard fortification on the river through the Highlands. The bulk of his army was ferried across the river to Haverstraw (about six miles north of the present-day Tappan Zee Bridge). From there he began his march to the Philadelphia area.

The exodus across the Hudson was none too soon because five days later, November 16, Howe ordered 8,000 of his men to attack Fort Washington, which was then manned by 3,000. The assault was so overwhelming that the colonel in command was forced to surrender after a short but valiant fight. Four days later Fort Lee was captured by a force of 4,000 men led by Lord Cornwallis. Except for leaving a number of troops to maintain control of the New Jersey side of the Hudson, Howe's army moved southward to occupy New Brunswick, Princeton, and Trenton before winter set in.

Meanwhile, to support Washington in his retreat, troops were being assembled for Generals Gates and Lee to attack Howe's army from the rear. For its part the New York Congress ordered Clinton to raise a detachment of militia from New York, New Jersey, and New England. Within days Clinton had assembled 1,200 men to join the expedition. Clinton's militia made a successful raid against a British stronghold near Bergen before being ordered back to Fort Montgomery.

STRATEGY CHANGE OF BRITISH WAR PLANS

With winter coming on, Clinton's return to Fort Montgomery found the threat of an invasion by

Howe's army considerably lessened. This situation became even more promising with news of Washington's winning the Battles of Trenton and Princeton. This turn of events led the military command in England to pursue Washington by ordering Howe to move the bulk of his army to the Philadelphia area. When Howe made the move in July, Sir Henry was left with 4,000 troops to occupy New York City.

Meanwhile, Gen. Burgoyne was mobilizing his army in Ticonderoga to advance to Albany, where he would join forces with Col. St. Leger's troops arriving from Canada via the St. Lawrence and Mohawk Rivers. Fortunately, this plan went awry because St. Leger's men were defeated by the Americans at Fort Stanwix (near present-day Rome). At the same time, Burgoyne was temporarily stalled after an indecisive battle at Bennington.

Upon learning about Burgoyne's invasion plans, the Continental Congress appointed Gen. Horatio Gates as commander of the Northern Department, with headquarters to be established in Albany. On orders from Washington to reinforce Gates's army, Clinton succeeded in sending 2,800 New York militia.

These were in addition to regular army personnel already sent, leaving only 1,200 Continentals and 300 militia for Gen. Putnam to defend Peekskill and only 800 men left to garrison both Fort Montgomery and Fort Clinton. Such was the situation on September 28 when Putnam learned that Sir Henry had received 3,000 additional troops from England, bringing his total strength to 7,000.

Within a few days after the arrival of his reinforcements, Sir Henry received a communiqué from the stranded Burgoyne appealing for assistance in way of a divisionary attack on Fort Montgomery. In response to this urgency, Sir Henry within four days organized an assault force of 3,000 troops that had sailed up the Hudson, arriving on October 5 at a point just four miles below Peekskill. With the enemy in such close proximity, Putnam was in a position of not knowing if he would be attacked, in which case he could not send reinforcements to Clinton at Fort Montgomery.

Sir Henry's strategy became clear early the next morning when 2,000 of his men crossed the river at a point only four miles below Fort Clinton and then climbed a passageway several hundred feet above the river. There, Sir Henry divided his forces for a simultaneous attack on both forts. When one of the assault teams came within striking distance of Fort Montgomery, its commander made a proposal for George Clinton to surrender. Upon refusal Clinton's small number of men manned the fort until it was overrun by the British. Meanwhile, the other assault group under the personal command of Sir Henry routed Fort Clinton's garrison after meeting a determined resistance. Gen. James Clinton suffered a serious bayonet wound on his thigh but managed to escape in the darkness. George Clinton was also fortunate in being able to escape with the other survivors.

Following these battles, Sir Henry's reorganized forces destroyed fortifications along the river before a contingent moved on to burn Kingston to the ground. Spaulding considered this sacking of the State's capital as "one of the most brutal, indefensible actions of the entire war."[8] It probably resulted in a more determined resolve for New Yorkers to fight for their independence.

What plans Sir Henry had for advancing northward after this episode are unknown because he soon learned of Burgoyne's surrender at Saratoga, thus prompting him to move his troops back to New York City.

Both Clinton and Putnam were questioned on what might have been done differently for a more defensive effort. But under the circumstances it has been agreed that the supreme action was taken. Washington added to this consensus when he wrote Clinton, "It is to be regretted that so brave a resistance did not meet with a suitable reward. You have however, the satisfaction of knowing that everything was done that could possibly be, by a handful against a far superior force."

CLINTON RESUMES HIS DUTIES AS GOVERNOR

Sir Henry's departure provided George Clinton with an interlude to conduct his governorship in a more orderly manner. Previously, he had returned only briefly from Fort Montgomery to the state capital in Kingston for legislative sessions.

As noted in the foreword, Clinton had been elected as New York's first governor on July 9, 1777. Because of his popularity among the rank and file, Clinton had the envious record of being elected governor and lieutenant governor simultaneously. He was well liked for being an early advocate of independence from England, and he was especially held in high esteem among militia members for his exemplary leadership.

Opposing him in the election were three candidates—Gen. Philip Schuyler of Albany being the leading one. Schuyler was from a distinguished family and had a fine war record that appealed mostly to conservatives. Another opponent, John Jay, who had been the main authority in drafting the state constitution, was not an avid candidate by token of his indicating a preference to become chief justice. Jay ended up backing Schuyler in hopes this support would cause Clinton to come in second. The third candidate was John Morin Scott, a brigadier general who had served in both the Continental and Provincial Congresses. According to Spaulding he was "too ardent a democrat and too fanatical a patriot to appeal to the moderates."[9] The voting gave Jay 367, Scott 368, Schuyler 1,199, and Clinton 1,828—Clinton amassing almost a majority. At the same time, Clinton was elected lieutenant governor by a substantial plurality, an office that he resigned.

After the election, Washington wrote, in a letter to the New York Convention:

> The appointment of General Clinton to the Government of your state is an event, that, in itself, gives me great pleasure, and very much abates the regret I should otherwise feel for the loss of his Services in the Military line. That Gentleman's Character is Such, as will make him peculiarly useful as the head of your State in a situation so alarming and interesting, as it at present experiences. For the future, agreeably to your desire, I shall direct my applications to him.

After the sacking of Kingston, the legislature moved to Poughkeepsie. The most immediate business was in organizing the new government's affairs in compliance with the new constitution. The New York State constitution, approved on April 20, 1777, was in some significant respects a precursor in the framing of the federal constitution ten years later. For example, New York's governor was to be elected by the people as opposed to being elected by the legislature. The governor in addition to being the commander-in-chief had the authority to convene the legislature, which also was adopted later by the federal government. The governor also had the authority to veto legislation but only with approval of the Council of Revision, consisting of the state's chancellor and three supreme court judges.

AND STILL ANOTHER CHANGE IN BRITAIN'S WAR STRATEGY

Once Sir Henry had retreated his forces to New York City in October 1777, the state of New York, except for an increasing number of raids on settlements along the Mohawk River by the

British, Indians, and Loyalist Tories, was free of military action until Sir Henry launched another assault up the Hudson in May 1779.

During this interval Gen. Howe had occupied Philadelphia, during which time he retired and was replaced by Sir Henry. Shortly afterward the British high command in a reversal of strategy concluded that the conquest of the Hudson and northward was mandatory for eventually winning the war. Toward that end, Sir Henry was ordered to move the main army in Philadelphia back to New York City. However, in one of the most crucial battles of the Revolution, Washington's army, rejuvenated after Valley Forge, intercepted Sir Henry's army at Monmouth, New Jersey. Although a standoff in casualties, Washington's out-maneuvering of Britain's main army gave more evidence that a victory could eventually be on the way.

After the battle, Washington marched his army through eastern New Jersey and then crossed the Hudson to West Point where it was stationed.

FIRST FRENCH MILITARY AID ARRIVES

Sir Henry lost no time in moving his army to New York City to defend against a possible invasion. The army marched to Sandy Hook at the entrance of the harbor, where it was transported by Adm. Howe's ships to the city. Had the army arrived just five days later, it would have been met at Sandy Hook by a French fleet commanded by Adm. Comte d'Estaing. However, although the French fleet could not have pursued Adm. Howe because the French vessels were too large to maneuver in the inner harbor, it would play a crucial role at Yorktown, Maryland, in the surrender of Cornwallis.

An earlier show of assistance to the Americans was the arrival of Lafayette, who personally provided a moral lift through his valor as a division commander at Monmouth. Lafayette contributed to a pro-American feeling in France and his influence may have helped to bring about a treaty with the United States in February 1778. Likewise, his influence may have led France to send Gen. Comte Rochambeau with his army of 5,500 troops to Rhode Island in 1780.

INTERNAL STATE MATTERS REQUIRE GOV. CLINTON'S ATTENTION

Once Washington's move to West Point had been made, measures were taken to refortify nearby Fort Constitution and to construct additional fortifications in and along the Hudson. This included the laying of a chain across the river as shown in Figure 6. This chain was considerably stronger than the one at Bear Mountain and was never tested by British vessels.

At this juncture the war had reached a stalemate in the north. The army at West Point had increased in size and had benefited from additional training, which resulted in a growing confidence to the extent that overtures were made to recapture New York City. However, Washington and his generals eventually decided that the timing and military situation were not feasible. These threats did, nevertheless, prevent Sir Henry from reinforcing Lord Cornwallis's operations in the South.

PROBLEMS WITH LOYALISTS IN NEW YORK CITY

Sir Henry Clinton's military occupation of the city was supported and assisted by the greatest concentration of Loyalists in the colonies. Their members included wealthy merchants and property owners who would be affected most by the war.

Once the Declaration of Independence was signed, about 100,000 colonists—about

West Point, as seen in the fall of 1778.

6. West Point, 1778. From Diamant, *Chaining the Hudson.* Used with permission.

3 percent of the total population—remained loyal to the king and left for England and British colonies. About 37,000 of these Loyalists went to Canada. Others remaining loyal were the 23,000 who joined the British army. Known as Tories, these men took up arms with Indians against independent settlers in New York and Pennsylvania.

The Declaration also terminated the connection between the Anglican churches and the Church of England. This termination ended England's financial support of the clergy, resulting in a vast reduction in their numbers, as detailed in James Bell's book on early Anglican churches.[10]

A more immediate and pressing problem was the dire financial situation for the state throughout the war. Before hostilities began financial dealings were handled mostly by paper money issued by the Colony. When it became obvious that the war could not be financed in this manner, Clinton proposed that taxation was necessary to bring in a greater supply of "hard cash." As a result, the legislature in March 1778 provided for the taxing of real and personal property, which added considerable cash through the sale of Loyalist property.

In addition to the scarcity of cash was the lack of foodstuffs, which became more acute because of a drought in the fall of 1779. The problem was compounded by the supplies of wheat and other grains being purchased in New York by New England states, which drove up the price and added to the scarcity of New York's own military and civilian needs.

3

The War Expands to the West

WESTERN NEW YORK BECOMES
A NEW BATTLEGROUND

The Declaration of Independence brought on another enemy: the Six Nations in alliance with the British Loyalists. In way of background, Sir William Johnson, New York's Indian agent, had worked out a treaty with the Indian tribes in 1769. This treaty was occasioned by the recapturing of English forts from the French, the Indians' former ally. Sir William's common-law wife was the sister of Joseph Brant, a Mohawk chief. Brant became the Indian agent's secretary after attending Dr. Eleazar Wheelock's Indian school, which was the forerunner of Dartmouth College.

The beginnings of the Revolutionary War gave the Six Nations the golden opportunity to align with the Loyalists against a common adversary. In the case of the Indian tribes, this could forestall the increasing westward movement by the colonists. Brant lost no time after the Declaration in leading an assault on Unadilla, a white settlement on the Susquehanna River.

The attack caused Gov. Clinton to have his intermediators try to convince Brant of the folly in the long run for an alliance with England. Lafayette joined in on these persuasions but to no avail because the Indians were already on the warpath and soon the entire frontier would be under attack. By May 1778

the burning of houses and barns and the destruction and stealing of crops and livestock had extended as far east as Schoharie, just 25 miles west of Albany.

At the same time, the aggression had moved south into the Susquehanna River valley in Pennsylvania. On July 3, 1778, in one of the bloodiest attacks of the war, the Connecticut Yankee settlers were overwhelmed in a surprise attack by Indian warriors. Known as the Wyoming Massacre, the survivors were aghast to learn that the Tories had paid the Indians for the 227 scalps extracted from the defenders. Then, four months later after a series of raids along the Mohawk, a force of 700 Tories and Indians laid waste to homes in a vicious assault at Cherry Valley, New York.

THE SULLIVAN-CLINTON CAMPAIGN

It became obvious to the Continental Congress that a special army was necessary to repel the combined enemy forces. Beyond saving settlers lives, a massive military campaign would preserve the farms needed for supplying foodstuffs to the Continental Army and at the same time halt the flow of such supplies to the British.

An overriding objective for a large military campaign was observed by the New York State historian, Alexander C. Fleck, in 1929, in a booklet commemorating the 200th anniversary of the expedition and containing a map

JOSEPH BRANT. THAYENDANEGEA.

THE GREAT CAPTAIN OF THE SIX NATIONS.

7. Joseph Brant (Thayendanegea). Engraving by A. Dick, from painting by G. Romney. Collection of The New-York Historical Society. Used with permission.

of it as reproduced in the description of the expedition:

> By 1779 . . . Washington and other leaders saw that independence with a mere fringe of land along the seacoast would scarcely be worth the cost of the struggle if the rest of the continent to the westward and northward remained in the hands of the motherland. Washington knew by practical experience the potential wealth of the fertile regions of the interior of the continent. He realized that when the time came to discuss the terms of peace that rich area could be secured for the young nation only if it was in possession of the Americans. The conquest of western New York, the capture of Oswego and Niagara and the seizure of posts farther west would assure American possession at the end of the war.[1]

Whatever may have been contained in Washington's appeal to the Continental Congress, the formation of a special army was authorized in February 1779. The importance of this undertaking was demonstrated by Washington's decision to allocate a third of the entire Continental army to pursue the objectives.

Formation of the Expedition

Washington's first step was to appoint Maj. Gen. John Sullivan to head the expedition. Sullivan had resigned his seat in Congress to enter the army at the outbreak of the Revolution and first served at Bunker Hill. Later he was a commander in Washington's successful victory at Trenton. At Monmouth, Sullivan helped intercept the British after replacing Gen. Charles Lee of his command. He was described by Chemung County historians, who contributed in the writing of the commemorative pamphlet, as "hot-headed, oversensitive, a born political organizer"—which may help

explain his differences with Washington on how to subdue the Six Nations.[2]

Gen. James Clinton was selected to serve the northern component of the expedition because of his knowledge of the area and his experience in warfare with both the Indians and the British, as discussed earlier.

After his appointment, Sullivan was ordered to organize an army of 3,500 seasoned troops made up of units from the Mid-Atlantic and New England states. The army would be formed and trained at Easton, Pennsylvania. His army would then proceed to Tioga Point, as shown on the map (Figure 8), where it would be met by Clinton's brigade. At that juncture plans would be made to make a combined assault on the enemy.

It took from February to mid-June for the army to get organized for a departure from Easton; they did not reach Tioga Point until August 11. The time consumed might be explained in part by Sullivan's procrastination; he wrote to Congress while the expedition was being organized that "the plan for carrying out the expedition was not agreeable to his mind, nor were the numbers of men destined for it, sufficient in his opinion to ensure success."

Sullivan's letter, which Washington stated was "for his own justification, in case of misfortune," put Washington in the delicate position of having to defend the ways he had ordered the campaign to be executed. This he did in a letter to Congress, dated August 15, 1779:

> The plan he [Sullivan] proposed, was to have two bodies, each superior to the whole force of the Enemy, to operate both to the Mohawk River and by way of the Susquehanna. This plan might have been desireable, if the number of our troops, the state of our finances and of our supplies had permitted its execution, but it was impracticable on all these accounts. The force actually detached, left the Army so weak, that I am persuaded every officer of reflection

in it, who knew our true circumstances, was uneasy for the consequences; and if a larger force had gone, we should have been absolutely at the discretion of the Enemy. This will immediately will appear from the recurrence to the returns of the Army at that time. Should we have endeavored to make up the deficiency from the Militia, our experience of the success of the applications which were made, will convince us that the attempt would have been fruitless; to say nothing of the injury to the agriculture which would have resulted from calling out so large a body of Militia. But if the men could have been procured we should have failed in supplies. This is evident from what has happened. If we have met with so many difficulties, disappointments and delays in providing for the *present force*, how would it have been possible to have provided for *double the number*?

Gen. James Clinton did not receive orders to move his brigade until late April because of the need for secrecy to keep the Indians guessing where and when his brigade might move. He was then informed that Canajoharie on the Mohawk would be the assembly location. During May and June the 1,600-man brigade would be engaged in building some 200 boats for transporting the troops down the Susquehanna. After moving to Lake Otsego (at Cooperstown) Clinton had a dam constructed to help buoy the boats down the river when the dam was broken. He then waited for more than a month for orders to descend down the river, finally meeting up with Sullivan at Tioga Point on August 22.

The Invasion Campaign Begins

Within ten days the Indian-Tory forces were sighted at Newtown (near Elmira) on the Chemung River. The enemy under the command of Capt. Joseph Brant consisted of a few British soldiers, two Tory Ranger battalions, and a large number of Cayugas, Mohicans, and Senecas.

Knowing that Sullivan's army had to advance along the lower ground near the river, the enemy's strategy was to fire on the Americans from the hills above and then to attack their rear. This strategy was countered by the contingents of Generals Clinton and Poor outflanking the enemy on higher ground and forcing the enemy warriors to turn in the direction of the artillery fire from the lower level. In this manner the enemy was contained for seven hours before retreating. Considering the numbers of men engaged on both sides, the losses of the Americans were minimal, 3 killed and 39 wounded.

Aftermath of the Campaign

Newtown was the first and last major engagement of the campaign. The defeat broke the morale of the Six Nations and ended whatever plans they may have had for making a stand to prevent Sullivan's advance into the Finger Lake region. During the next 30 days before the conclusion of the campaign, the Sullivan-Clinton forces had destroyed 40 Indian towns and demolished large quantities of foodstuffs.

Whatever ideas Sullivan may have had in mind for wanting to make an assault on Fort Niagara could never have come to pass because the army at that point did not have provisions for the estimated two weeks that would have been involved.

An ongoing result of the expedition was the releasing of some 4,000 men and their equipment and supplies for use elsewhere. In part, Gen. Clinton's brigade would be reformed to join Comte de Rochambeau's corps of 5,500 French soldiers stationed in Rhode Island before its march to Yorktown where Cornwallis was forced to surrender.

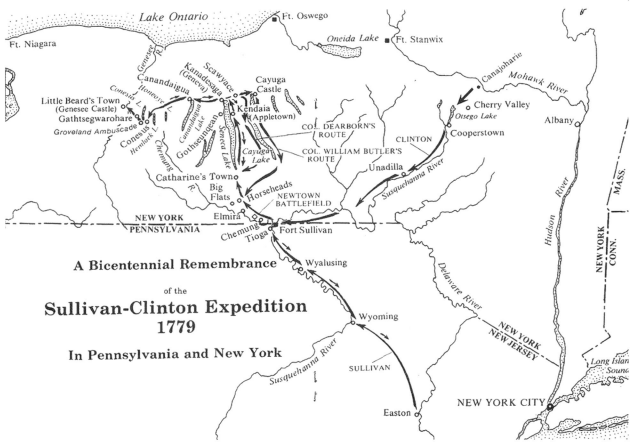

8. Map of the Sullivan-Clinton campaign. From "Against the Iroquois," 1929.

PROBLEMS ERUPT AGAIN
ON THE FRONTIER

In his role as governor during the Sullivan-Clinton Expedition, George Clinton was involved in a variety of administrative matters pertaining to the expedition. The success of its outcome added recognition to the already popular governor. In Clinton's run for reelection in 1780, Schuyler was no more of a factor than before and Jay was out of the running because he was on a diplomatic mission in Spain. Consequently, Clinton won by a wide margin in the May 1780 election.

The reelected governor was soon faced with another uprising on the frontier. This time the Indians and Tories were in a state of revenge after their members had been been so thoroughly subdued at Newtown. Under the leadership of Sir John Johnson a series of border raids began with 700 troops transported from Montreal to the Mohawk River just some 20 miles west of Schenectady. When Clinton learned of this foray, he personally led his militia in an attempt to cut off Sir John's retreat but was too late in the pursuit.

Clinton was concerned that the enemy would regroup and attack in another area. His premonition was proven when he learned from Washington about Benedict Arnold's treason. Having been the commander at West Point, Arnold deserted his command there to join the Tory forces in Canada. Soon after, Sir John, again leading a raiding contingent, sailed from Canada on Lake Ontario to Oswego. From there his troops traveled along the Mohawk

9. Map of the New York and Vermont disputed areas.

to Schoharie, where the troops began laying waste to the countryside. The situation became so devastating that Clinton again took personal command of the militia to assist Gen. Robert Van Rensselaer, who needed help in pursuing the enemy. Although Sir John's troops managed to escape, Clinton's counterattack saw the last of raiding. The end of the raiding also marked the end of military action within the state. By that time the battleground had moved to the southern states, and the surrender of Cornwallis took place in October 1781.

NEW YORK IS FACED WITH BOUNDARY PROBLEMS

The surrender of British forces immediately brought up the question of whether lands in New York's western frontier belonged to the state or to the government represented by Congress. Except for the disputed area involving Vermont,[3] New York's boundaries were mostly defined as bordering New Jersey and Pennsylvania on the south and the southern shores of Lake Ontario and the St. Lawrence River on the north. When considering the distances that would be involved in administering New York's western land claims, Justice Jay and Robert R. Livingston, the state's delegate to Congress, recommended ceding the claims to Congress.

Gov. Clinton was in favor of this proposal provided that Virginia also cede its claims. However, Virginia insisted on retaining jurisdiction over lands claimed north of the Ohio River. Clinton's opposition to this provision resulted in its removal by Congress in 1782.

VERMONT STATEHOOD IS FINALLY SETTLED

Clinton's inheritance of the Vermont problem went back to 1749 when the governor of New Hampshire repudiated the claims by New York for lands west of the Connecticut River. New York later based its claims on an edict issued by the "king in council" in 1764. During this interval, settlers, largely from Connecticut and Massachusetts, were given title to their land under what became known as "the New Hampshire Grants." At the same time, in addition to New York settlers, prominent men including

George Clinton and John Jay were given large grants of land in recognition of their services to New York.

The dispute came to a head in January 1775 when Vermont was proclaimed a state by Ethan Allen and his Green Mountain Boys, who had earlier captured Fort Ticonderoga on Lake Champlain. The Allens and their associates had likewise purchased land in the disputed area.

When Clinton became governor he was faced with the problem of how to resolve the conflict. As a landowner in the area he was involved in a conflict of interest. Kaminski noted some of the underlying factors when he stated that "Clinton had a blind spot when it came to Vermont. He never saw the parallel between Vermont's struggle for independence and America's. Vermonters, in his judgment, were traitors who had taken 'ungenerous Advantage of our Situation' to secede from the state. As governor, Clinton was sworn to protect and defend his state and the rights and property of its citizens. The Vermont insurgents violated these rights and struck at the core of New York's sovereignty."[4]

Nevertheless, dealing with the realities of the situation, Clinton was hopeful that a peaceful settlement could be achieved. His immediate concerns were for the welfare of New Yorkers already in residence in the disputed area. Toward that end he issued a proclamation in February 1778 offering to give title to settlers from other states providing they accept New York's sovereignty. After this proposal was met by outright refusal, Clinton offered to have the dispute settled by Congress if the grants would come under New York's jurisdiction. The refusal this time resulted in a military skirmish by Ethan Allen in Brattleboro, precipitating Congress to send a committee to the area. When only two members responded, the New York senate voted to work out terms of jurisdiction with representatives of Vermont, which in itself would be an admission of Vermont statehood. Because the Assembly did not agree with the Senate's approach, the dispute carried on for nearly nine years until 1790 when New York recognized Vermont as being a state. A year later Vermont adopted the U.S. Constitution and became the 14th state.

4

New York after Cornwallis's Surrender

CLINTON ENJOYS WAR HERO STATUS

The end of hostilities brought a short period of prosperity to New York that was followed by a depression just two years later beginning in 1785. In the interval, however, Clinton was able to bask in what Spaulding described as being "at the height of his fame, perhaps at the zenith of his career. He was everywhere recognized as one of the foremost heroes of the war and as one of the most capable of the war governors."[1]

The interval also provided time for Clinton to be with his friend George Washington, who was then stationed with his army at Newburg, just a short distance from the Clinton family seat at New Windsor. From May through the fall of 1782 both men toured the Hudson Highland area to assess the damage that had been inflicted and decide upon means of reconstruction. Then, in 1783, from July 18 to August 5, they spent three weeks touring upstate New York in search of land they could buy. Following are excerpts from an account of this trip by Kaminski in *The Governor and the Commander in Chief: A Study in Admiration and Friendship*:

> They travelled more than 750 miles together throughout the frontier making a list of potential tracts. Later the governor made bids on the property. . . . Clinton purchased 6,071 acres on the Mohawk

River . . . a few miles southwest of Utica. Washington complimented Clinton on the "advantageous terms in the purchase . . . you certainly have obtained it amazingly cheap." Although the land was shared equally, Clinton paid for it with his own money, charging Washington seven percent annual interest on his debt. In December 1783 Washington arranged for over $2,000 owed to him by the Confederation government to be transferred from the federal treasury to Clinton as the first installment on his debt. A second payment was made in April 1785. In November 1786 Washington informed Clinton that he was "endeavouring by the sale of the Land, to raise money for my Moiety of the purchase on the Mohawk River," and the following June Washington paid the balance of $840. . . . On February 28, 1796 Washington wrote Clinton asking what lots remained unsold in their joint venture. A week later Clinton informed his partner that they still owned seven lots consisting of 1,446 acres valued at over five dollars per acre. Clinton recommended that the land not be sold. "The soil is good and in proportion to the rapid settlement of that Part of the Country the value of those Lands continue to increase." With almost twenty-five percent of their land still available, the investment had already returned a handsome investment. The two old surveyors had done well as a team.[2]

CELEBRATING THE EVACUATION OF NEW YORK CITY

Cornwallis's surrender was followed by the Treaty of Paris in November 1782 and ratified the following April by the United States. This treaty provided for, among other important conditions, the withdrawal of all British military forces "with all convenient speed." For Gov. Clinton this meant prompt collaborations with Sir Guy Carleton, the British commander-in-chief. Sir Guy, however, proved to be evasive about removal of troops from Westchester County, Long Island, and New York City. Washington had to add his weight to bring about faster action. Even so, it was not until November 25, 1783, before the removal of troops culminated in the triumphal reoccupation of New York City by the Americans.

With the last British troops having left the city, the long-awaited day was celebrated first of all with the raising of the American flag on a newly erected pole at the reoccupied fort. Then, a 13-gun salute signaled the entry procession with Washington and Clinton side by side on horseback, led by members of West Chester's light cavalry.

The day's activities were culminated by a grand dinner at Fraunces Tavern given by Clinton for Washington and his officers. The governor hosted another dinner on December 1 honoring Washington and the French minister, the Chevalier de la Luzerne. New Yorkers enjoyed a gala fireworks display the same evening.

WASHINGTON-CLINTON RELATIONSHIP CARRIES ON

When Washington returned to Mt. Vernon, where he planned to spend his retirement, he wrote Clinton the following letter on December 28, 1783:

I am now a private citizen on the banks of the Potomack, where I should be happy to see you, if your public business would ever permit, and where in the meantime I shall fondly cherish the remembrance of all your former friendship. Although I scarcely need tell you how much I have been satisfied with every instance of your public conduct, yet I could not suffer Col. Walker . . . to depart for New York without giving your candidacy one more testimony of the obligations I consider myself under for the spirited and able assistance, I have often derived from the State under your administration. The scene is at last closed—I find myself eased of a load of public care—I hope to spend the remainder of my days in cultivating the affections of good men, and in the practice of the domestic virtues. Permit me then to consider you in the number of my friends, and to wish you every felicity. Mrs. Washington joins me in presenting the compliments of the season, with our best respects to Mrs. Clinton and the family.

This letter was followed up in part by Clinton sending Washington an assortment of trees for transplanting at Mount Vernon. And, knowing of Washington's interest in plant experimentation, Clinton arranged for shipments of a variety of vegetable seeds and nursery plants.

NEW YORK CITY BECOMES THE HUB OF POLITICAL ACTIVITY

Just a few months after the city was free of British troops, the New York legislature met there and continued to do so until it moved to Albany when it became the state capital in 1801. By the same token, the Clinton family moved from Poughkeepsie to the city in 1784 and remained in the vicinity until moving to the new capital.

10. The civil procession, headed by General Washington and Governor Clinton. Library of Congress LC-USZ62–13459.

The city was also the meeting place of the Continental Congress, which met there several times before the federal Constitution was adopted. It then had the honor of being selected as the site of the nation's first capital. Washington was sworn in as the first president of the United States on April 30, 1789, at Federal Hall on Wall St. Later on, several other cities served as the nation's capital until Washington, D.C., became the permanent site.

Clinton's popularity remained to the extent that he was reelected governor in 1783 and again in 1786—the latter reelection even with a financial depression that became critical by 1785.

CLINTON DEALS WITH FINANCIAL CRISIS THAT SPREADS THROUGHOUT THE NATION

Following the war a period of relative good economic conditions prevailed as those in the military returning home performed their previous and other tasks. By the mid 1780s, however, a series of financial conditions set in that brought the economy to a near standstill. The most overriding problem had been the growing scarcity of money, whether it be in the form of "paper" issued by the states and Congress or coin. This in turn brought on an increasing amount of public and personal debt and the lack of funds for domestic and foreign trade.

Throughout the depressed conditions New York had fared better than most states because of fiscal measures instituted by Clinton early in his administrations. Revenues from a tariff on goods passing through its seaports were used in helping to keep taxes to a minimum and for paying for such services as building roads to foster trade. Tax revenues were also used to subsidize public education to lessen family financial burdens. It is no wonder Clinton was such a popular governor.

With regard to the scarcity of paper money, Clinton refrained from its issuance except in most dire circumstances. For many, however, economic conditions had reached the point where Assembly members succeeded several times in authorizing the issuance of paper certificates only to have the Senate defeat passage of the bills. Finally, by March 6, 1786, a bill providing for the issuance of certificates in an amount acceptable to Clinton was passed. The new bill contained much of Clinton's recommendations by having three-fourths of the issue earmarked for mortgage and real estate transactions. The remainder was for use in paying taxes and interest on state and continental securities.

5

Forming the Federal Government

**THE DECISIVE BATTLE IN FORMING
A NEW GOVERNMENT, WITH GEORGE
CLINTON IN THE FOREFRONT**

Adverse conditions experienced throughout all of the states because of the financial depression brought on a clamoring for the state assemblies to help deal with the situation. This unrest concerned the problem with debtor relief as provided by the assemblies, which resulted in a strong desire by many for Congress to restrict such action by the states.

George Clinton was very much behind a needed change because of the problems he had encountered in dealing with Congress. One such case was his belief that Congress should have supported New York's just claim that the Vermont territory was within the state's boundaries instead of granting Vermont statehood. Clinton also believed that Congress should have decreed that New York retain property rights for the land in western New York that Massachusetts had claimed under its charter of 1629. Because of such decisions detrimental to the interests of New York, Clinton wanted to ensure that any change in government would provide for protecting states' rights.

The first organized effort toward revising the Articles of Confederation took place in November 1780 when delegates from New England and New York met in Hartford to consider having Congress collect duties on foreign goods to pay for the war debt. After considerable discussion of the pros and cons the proposal was defeated.

Nothing more was formally organized until the Annapolis Convention of 1786, attended by delegates from Virginia, Delaware, Pennsylvania, New Jersey, and New York. While nothing of substance was decided upon at Annapolis, discussions later on of the convention's report led Congress to accept a motion on February 21, 1787, from the Massachusetts delegation to call for a Federal Convention wherein representatives from all the states would be authorized to draw up a new Constitution.

In the ensuing Convention that met for the first time in May 1787, the deliberations at Annapolis helped to bring into focus how a revised or new national government might be structured and the authority it would command. Some of the basic views expressed on these matters went back to the end of the war. Men such as Patrick Henry, Richard Henry Lee, and James Monroe believed that a consolidated national government was a dangerous threat to civil liberty. Others like George Clinton were concerned, as previously discussed, with the scope of the authority that a new government might have. Moreover, as observed in the following excerpt from Spaulding's biography, Clinton's beliefs were considerably more deep-rooted:

To George Clinton and his Anti-Federalist friends a strong centralized government represented the direct antithesis of all they had fought for in the Revolution. They did not wish to be governed from a far-away capital, taxed by the representatives of other states, and disciplined by standing armies over which they had little or no control. These were just the things that they had objected to under British rule and they wanted no more of them. Wars might have to be fought by federal armies, and treaties negotiated by the agents of a distant Congress; but most of the functions of government could be far better and more safely conducted by their own representatives in the city council or state legislature. They wished to be ruled by their own neighbors in their own state, not by the representatives of a dozen other states gathered at a distant capital. Why was it necessary to create a super state? After all, the federation had succeeded in winning a major war.[1]

ALEXANDER HAMILTON BECOMES LEADER OF THE FEDERALIST PARTY

It is ironic that Clinton's early friend and fellow New Yorker would soon become the Federalist's most recognized leader. Hamilton had advanced steadily in state politics after marrying the daughter of Gen. Philip Schuyler, Clinton's chief adversary.

Descended from Scottish nobility on his father's side, Hamilton was born and reared in British Caribbean possessions until leaving in 1772 when he was seventeen to pursue his education in America. His studies at Kings College, the forerunner of Columbia, were interrupted after the Boston Tea Party by his writing of pamphlets attacking British policy, which gained favorable attention of revolutionary leaders, including members of the New York legislature, who in 1776 made him a captain in the provincial artillery. After Hamilton had demonstrated his military ability and bravery at the battle of Trenton, Washington made him his aide-de-camp with the rank of lieutenant colonel.

It was at this time that Clinton got to know Hamilton—to the extent of Clinton being in charge of providing medical assistance to Hamilton in combating a serious illness. When he had recovered, Clinton recommended to Washington that Hamilton be placed in command of the Continental army along the Hudson. This friendship increased as both men were advocating a stronger Congress to deal with conducting the war—not realizing, of course, what would take place between them politically once the war was over.

Kaminski has observed that their relationship began to deteriorate after Hamilton was married and started to champion the causes of Schuyler, Jay, and others of moneyed interests.[2] Soon there was a difference among New Yorkers on how to improve economic conditions. As noted earlier, through implementation of Clinton's fiscal measures, New York had attained economic sufficiency as compared with other states. On the other hand, Hamilton in a move to combat near-worthless money elsewhere, proposed in 1780, the year of his marriage, the establishment of a central government bank. Such a bank would issue its notes by calling in outstanding notes of state and local banks. While this proposal for making a more stable currency did not meet with Congress's approval, it did make all concerned aware of Hamilton's advocacy for a strong central government.

In addition to the growing differences between Clinton and Hamilton on the role of the powers of the federal government versus those of the states were the day-to-day dealings with the Loyalists. While Hamilton was displaying an accommodation in the handling of Loyalists involved with others of moneyed interests, Clinton was staunchly behind disenfranchising the Loyalists but treating them considerately in the process.

Such was the situation between these men when delegates from New York were to be selected to attend the Federal Convention.

PROCEEDINGS OF THE FEDERAL CONVENTION

The selection of delegates to the convention proved to be an exercise in political maneuvering. In order to ensure as much as possible the selection of a majority of Anti-Federalist delegates, Clinton was in hopes of having New York be represented by three delegates. When the voting of the 52 assemblymen took place, all voted for Chief Justice Robert Yates. While Hamilton was chosen by a near unanimous vote, the selection of the third delegate was won by the mayor of Albany, John Lansing Jr., in a close race over the mayor of New York City, James Duane, a Federalist. Thus, Hamilton would be confronted with Yates and Lansing, both Anti-Federalists.

Shortly after the convention convened in Philadelphia on May 25, 1787, almost all of the delegates agreed on the need for a stronger national government. At the same time there was no consensus on what would be entailed in forming a new government and the authority it would have. Then, on June 18 in a speech lasting several hours Hamilton argued that a new government should be patterned after the one currently in use in England. He went on to elaborate on the functions of a chief executive with life tenure and a congress consisting of representatives with three-year terms and senators with life tenure.

Clinton's earlier misgivings about Hamilton's ideas for a strong national government were more than justified upon learning of such drastic proposals for a concentrated and continuing power that would be a threat to states' rights. Despite expressions for states'

rights by the New York delegates, the other state delegates in a successful exchange of ideas drafted a constitution which in its basic form was virtually identical to our present one, with the few changes in the amendments. This monumental work was completed in less than four months and was approved by the other states. This action, however, was just the first step because each state then had to go through the process of ratifying the Constitution.

As a first step in his groundwork to persuade New York to ratify the Constitution, Hamilton arranged for New York's newspaper, the *Daily Advertiser*, to print a copy of the Constitution and for an editorial advocating its adoption. To combat this publicity the Clintonians began a series of essays appearing every two weeks in the *New York Journal*. The basic themes of these essays, signed by "Cato," espoused the pitfalls to New York if the Constitution were to be adopted as then written and, therefore, the need for the formation of a federation of states with limited powers. Although, according to Kaminski, the authorship of the essays was never determined, it was generally assumed that they were written by Clinton.[3] Whoever the author, the essays initiated a vital addition to the Constitution through their proposal of the inclusion of the Bill of Rights, which spelled out Clinton's basic belief as a preface to the politically oriented instrument. This proposal may have influenced Jefferson to the extent of persuading Madison to make this addition, pointing out that a Bill of Rights would help gain support for adoption of the Constitution.

The Cato essays began a battle of accusations between the two factions when a letter appeared in the *Daily Advertiser* and signed by "Caesar"—soon to be thought by many as being Hamilton—accused the Anti-Federalists of playing dirty politics in making their appeals. This was followed by both Cato and Caesar resorting to unbecoming statements. When recognizing that this airing in the press was not promoting his cause, Hamilton enlisted the support of John Jay and James Madison to begin writing a series of essays explaining in persuasive terms how national and foreign affairs could better be handled under the Constitution as written. Between October 27, 1787, and May 28, 1788, 85 essays, 51 of which were attributed to Hamilton, appeared in various publications, soon becoming known as the Federalist Papers. The papers, which experienced a wide and favorable reception, were in time recognized as distinguished writings of political literature. Not only would they later on serve to help shape American political institutions, but more immediately they would promote Hamilton as the most recognized figure in the forming of the new government.

Despite the effect the Federalist Papers were having in swaying opinion, Clinton was hopeful that other states would not adopt the Constitution so that it would be unnecessary for New York to make a decision. Nevertheless, Clinton realized that he needed to bring the adoption matter before the legislature, which he did on January 11, 1788.

After several weeks of delay the legislature decided to hold a vote in naming delegates to make the adoption decision. Although Clintonians had 46 of the 65 Assembly seats in the previous election, Anti-Federalist support began waning by the time the legislature met in Poughkeepsie in June. Consequently, the convention delegation voted 30 to 27 for adoption after recognizing the definite unlikelihood of having the other states accept their proposed amendments. For Clinton this meant taking up the task of attaining what he could for states' rights during the process of forming the new government.

6

Involvement in National Affairs

CLINTON CONSIDERED FOR NATION'S FIRST VICE PRESIDENT

While Hamilton was being recognized as the dominant Federalist leader, historians of the period seem to have glossed over the fact that George Clinton at the same time was becoming nationally recognized as the main spokesman against the Constitution but also the one most likely to succeed in having amendments made to protect the interests of the states. Evidence of this reputation soon emerged when Virginia politicians started promoting Clinton for vice president early in the selection of electors for the first national general election. This backing was the beginning of a Republican political alliance between Virginia and New York that would continue until conditions changed as discussed later.

Kaminski, in his Clinton biography, deserves credit for detailing the thinking that was going on among those of political influence concerning the vital importance in selecting the vice president. In that capacity the one chosen could help "determine the future constitutional development of America."[1] This realization came into play more than ever when Washington, thought of as the unanimous choice for the presidency, let it be known that while he did not want the office he would accept with the condition he would not serve a complete term. This provision added to the

urgency in the selection of the most influential person as vice president and one who could become president after a short interval.

When selection of federal electors was getting underway the first to receive national attention was John Hancock, the former president of the Continental Congress and governor of Massachusetts. Hancock, however, failed to gain sufficient support from Federalist leaders because of his advocating amendments to the Constitution inconsistent with the Federalist cause. John Adams, also well known in Massachusetts, was then promoted as the most likely candidate. Several other states were also promoting their favorite sons, including George Clinton, who appeared to be the logical choice by Anti-Federalists in other states as well.

Supporters of Clinton began a campaign on his behalf on October 30 at Fraunces Tavern to form the Federal Republican Committee. While the term "republican" had been used in connection with Anti-Federalism, this was perhaps the first time it was used in a formal way as the name for this emerging political party. Whatever the case, Republican became established by the time Jefferson became associated with the name.

The Republican Committee prepared a circular addressing the need for a vice president to promote amendments to the Constitution that would secure the liberties for all Americans. The circular went on to state that the committee had been working with Virginia Anti-Federalists who were electioneering for Clinton. This ground swell for Clinton caused the partisan Philadelphia *Federal Gazette* in December to begin warning its readers about the threat that Clinton posed if elected and characterized him as having neither the "dignity nor understanding fit for that important station."[2] Other newspapers throughout the states were encouraged to reprint the *Gazette* articles.

Concern over Clinton running for office became so extensive that Federalists started spreading the rumor that Patrick Henry was opting for the presidency with Clinton as his running mate. Henry was such an extreme zealot in the cause of liberty that Federalists hoped that such a contrived association would be detrimental to Clinton's popularity.

Despite such tactics in maligning Clinton, his popularity among government people in other states was so strong that some Federalist leaders in the South began proposing John Adams as a northerner who could defeat Clinton. This development opened the door for Hamilton to also endorse Adams so as to present a united Federalist candidate. In so doing, however, Hamilton was caught in the uncertainty of what could take place when the electors cast their ballots. This uncertainty came about through the Constitution giving the electors two votes apiece to be cast as the choice for president with the runner-up becoming vice president. Consequently, Hamilton became worried that Adams with his strong Federalist ties might garner more votes than Washington, who was known for his more moderate political leanings. Such an outcome would present an uncertain political future for the Federalists. So concerned was Hamilton about this possible eventuality that he approached a number of electors to request they refrain from voting for Adams. Hamilton need not have worried about the outcome because when the ballots were cast, Washington was elected unanimously; Adams received 34 votes and the remaining 35 were split among ten other candidates.

Although the election had been held on February 4, 1789, it was not until April 23 that Washington arrived in New York City, the nation's first capital. Crossing the Hudson on a beautifully decorated 13-oared vessel, the new president was met by the city's prominent citizens, led by Clinton. During the week leading up to the inauguration Washington and Clinton resumed their personal relationship midst the entertaining and festivities.

A RUN FOR FIFTH TERM AS GOVERNOR

Washington's inaugural happened on the same day New Yorkers were at the polls for the gubernatorial election. On February 11, 1789, one week after Washington had been elected, Hamilton had initiated a campaign to have Clinton defeated in the upcoming election for governor in April. Hamilton had lost no time in wanting to prove that he was the dominant political leader of New York State. Again, Hamilton went on the attack with a series of letters printed in the *Daily Advertiser* that were signed "H.G." This time the letters were promoting Judge Robert Yates for governor. Yates, the former Anti-Federalist, was a strategic candidate to embrace both political factions because he had converted to the Federalist cause as soon as New York had ratified the Constitution.

But this time Hamilton's letters contained a considerably more sinister and derogatory characterization of Clinton. In fact, this unrestrained assault revealed Hamilton being consumed in his utter frustration over Clinton's continuing popularity. In explaining such behavior, Ron Chernow, in his biography *Alexander Hamilton*, attributed it perhaps to "a legacy of his troubled upbringing."[3] In his analysis of the "H.G." letters Chernow made the following observations, including excerpts he culled from the letters appearing in the New York City *Daily Advertiser*, which are shown in quotes:

> Reviewing the governor's political and military career, Hamilton accused him of "narrow views, a prejudiced and contracted disposition, a passionate and interested temper." He questioned Clinton's bravery as a brigadier general during the Revolution: "After diligent enquiry, I have not been able to learn that he was ever more than once in actual combat." . . . Hamilton accused Clinton of having stolen from Philip Schuyler the first governor's race, which was held during the Revolution, by forcing militiamen under his command to vote for him.[4]

Following a bitter campaign struggle Clinton was reelected but by a mere 429 votes. Although the Federalists won both branches of the legislature, Clinton, as governor, could wield his appointive powers to gain as much political control as possible.

Clinton lost no time to begin his political maneuverings by appointing some of his former adversaries into distinguished state positions, thereby hoping to gain in return their support on other matters. Among such appointments were those of Judge Yates and Aaron Burr, who had supported Yates in the gubernatorial election against Clinton. Yates was made the state's chief justice and Burr was made the state attorney general.

The Clintonians, together with a conservative faction of the Livingstons who opposed some of Hamilton's fiscal policies, agreed that Burr would be a popular candidate. The prediction proved right because the senate voted 14 to 4 for Burr. This vote marked the beginning of the feud between Hamilton and Burr. Hamilton became most distraught, not only that a thirty-four-year-old Burr would have the audacity to take on the reelection bid of Philip Schuyler, Hamilton's eminent father-in-law, but then by having to witness Burr winning convincingly.

HAMILTON'S FISCAL PROGRAM IS RESISTED

As the functioning of the new national government was getting underway, Hamilton as the newly appointed Secretary of the Treasury began outlining his plan to deal with the federal debt incurred before the Constitution and for paying off the war debt. In dealing with the federal debt Hamilton proposed funding it with interest-bearing securities. Clinton had reservations because it would be the wealthy—New York Federalists making up a large percentage of them—who would benefit mostly through their trading the securities.

As for the war debt, Hamilton proposed that the federal government assume the debt owed by all of the states. Again, Clinton had reservations because such an event would pave the way for financial speculation resulting from the trading of notes that had been purchased from the various states at a low price so as to receive a greater amount back from the government.

Concurrent with settling the debt problems were the debates in Congress for two years about the establishment of the Bank of the United States that came about in July 1791. As discussed previously, Clinton was opposed to such a bank that could issue a federal currency and thereby diminish the widespread use of state currency and its effect on the state's ability to handle its own fiscal matters. Despite Clinton's misgivings, the New York legislature voted to subscribe to shares of the new federal bank. Moreover, the legislature authorized the chartering of independent banks, which Clinton was opposed to because he believed they would primarily benefit merchants while making high-interest loans to others or no loans at all to farmers.

11. "First in Peace." Color lithograph representing the arrival of General George Washington at the Battery, New York, April 23, 1789. Collection of The New-York Historical Society. Used with permission.

CLINTON UP AGAIN FOR REELECTION IN 1792

During his previous three-year term there had been inroads in lessening Clinton's vote-getting proficiency. Namely, this was caused by the number of New Englanders who settled in western New York and those changing over to the Federalist cause now that the Constitution was becoming established. These developments led the Federalists to believe Chief Justice Yates was their best candidate. But Yates announced that he would not be a candidate because the office did not meet his financial requirements. Actually, Yates withdrew because Aaron Burr had confided that he himself wanted the governorship. With Yates not running the Federalists succeeded in enlisting Chief Justice John Jay as their candidate. Burr then withdrew from the race after realizing the loss of needed backing.

Considerable electioneering followed with the Schuyler group trying to enlist the conservative Livingston faction, which was undecided because of the need for Clinton's help in obtaining approval of their land grants, but as it turned out he did not have to deal with that. The Livingstons were upset because their family had received no jobs under Washington's administration. They also backed Clinton's successful effort to replace Schuyler with Burr as U.S. senator.

The election began on April 24 with five days for balloting. This was followed by a four-week interval before ballot counting. At first it was believed that Jay had won. But then the contesting of the counting procedure caused the voting to be close. Finally, it was agreed that the votes in three pivotal counties be discarded. This action left Clinton as the winner with 8,457 over Jay's 8,315.

The aftermath became bitter when Clintonians were accused of stealing the election combined with appeals that Clinton should resign. This was followed by Federalist efforts to have the election invalidated. However, when the legislature convened, the Republicans—as Clintonians were then calling themselves—came up with a small but decisive majority for Clinton, thus ending any further action to discredit the election.

ANOTHER RUN FOR THE U.S. VICE PRESIDENCY

No sooner had Clinton lost his bid for the office of vice president in January 1789 than the Federalists expressed concerns of his running the next time. Hamilton in June of that year confided with Adams that Clinton would be his main competitor. And Pennsylvania politicians were so worried that they encouraged their governor to run and disrupt Clinton's popularity.

Added to these concerns were a series of articles in September 1789 in the *New York Journal* promoting Clinton's candidacy. Signed by "A Citizen" the series recommended Clinton as the Republican who could best defeat Adams, who was described as a tyrant who favored the aristocracy.[5] During this series the political situation took on an eventful turn with Aaron Burr's announcement that as a Republican he would accept a nomination for the office. Thus, Burr's candidacy presented a double concern to the Federalists because he had the backing of influential Republicans in New England, New York, and Pennsylvania. If Jefferson should support Burr, the resulting pressure might cause Adams to withdraw from the race. More immediately, the prospects prompted Clinton to let it be known that he did not wish to run.

These developments led to one of the most bizarre scenarios in early American politicking when Hamilton was caught again in a precarious situation—this time when his dislike of Burr was so intense that he was forced to back Clinton, his nemesis long before Burr came on the scene. While admitting that Clinton was "opposed to national principles," he was, on the other hand, "a man of property, and, in private life" a man "of probity." Hamilton went on the attack of Burr by branding him as too young and without the experience to run against Adams. In further comments culled by Kaminski, Hamilton demeaned Burr as "unprincipled both as a public and private man. . . . He is for or against nothing, but as it suits his interest or ambition. He is determined, as I conceive, to make his way to be head of the popular party and to climb per *fas et nefas* [legally or illegally] to the highest honors of the state; and as much higher as circumstances may permit."[6]

Hamilton's diatribes could well have had an effect on the outcome of an October 16 meeting of Republican leaders in Philadelphia to endorse their support for Clinton. Kaminski observed that although there is no evidence that Jefferson attended the meeting, Jefferson, nonetheless, was knowledgeable of what was going on. Moreover, Kaminski further observed, "Because of the broad representation at this meeting, it might well be viewed as the birth of a national Republican party organization."[7] The playback of this meeting in behalf of Clinton was sufficient for Burr to bow out of contention.

But another overriding aspect was taking place and that was the recognition that nationwide Republicans recognized Jefferson as their preference to take on Adams. Again, provisions of the Constitution got in the way of such a development. In this instance presidential electors were prohibited from casting both of their ballots for candidates from their home states. In view of Virginia's 21 electors committed to Washington, Jefferson's chances for the vice presidency were remote.

When the presidential electors cast their ballots on December 5, 1792, Washington and Adams were reelected, with Clinton receiving 50 votes to Adams's 77. Clinton won unanimously in New York, Virginia, North Carolina, and Georgia but did not do well in New England and Pennsylvania.

EFFECTS OF THE FRENCH REVOLUTION

The bitter campaign leading to Clinton's sixth term substantially narrowed support for the governor in view of the Federalists gaining the majority of the seats in the state legislature in the 1793 election. By the time of this election national attention was being focused on the aftermath of the French Revolution which was causing serious social unrest in parts of Europe and beginning to cause an upheaval in American politics.

The revolution had gained the sympathies of New York Republicans who looked upon the rebellion in the same light of the American colonies overthrowing their oppressors and gaining independence from England. This allegiance led to an awkward situation, however, when France began using American seaports to accommodate their warships—thereby threatening the neutrality of the United States. Recognizing that such activities on New York shores could lead to serious consequences, Clinton informed the legislature in January 1793 that he had been requested by federal authorities to curb belligerent activities of both France and Great Britain. Then in May, two weeks after Washington's Neutrality Proclamation was publicized, Clinton issued his own proclamation resulting in the seizure of French warships in New York harbors, which were turned over to federal custody. In appreciation of such action, Washington asked Hamilton to draft a letter thanking New Yorkers for their support. In this letter, which Hamilton reluctantly composed, Clinton was also acknowledged for his part to "harmonize and invigorate all parts of our political system."

THE GENÊT AFFAIR TURNS INTO A CLINTON FAMILY AFFAIR

The matter of neutrality took on sinister circumstances with the arrival in Charleston in April 1793 of Edmond Genêt as the new French minister to the United States. In addition to his instructions to receive payments for the Revolutionary War debt owed to France, Genêt could use these funds to provide military supplies for striking blows against British and Spanish possessions in North America.

In the view of Chernow as expressed in his *Alexander Hamilton,* Jefferson by assisting these endeavors was violating the neutrality proclamation.[8] Nevertheless, Jefferson and Republicans in Pennsylvania and New York welcomed Genêt with open arms as representing a true spirit of liberty as opposed to Federalist overtures still being associated with the aristocracy. By the time Genêt had traveled northward to New York he was being hailed as "Citizen" Genêt.

At one of the receptions for celebrating the tenth anniversary of Britain's evacuation of New York City, the thirty-three-year-old Genêt met Cornelia, the nineteen-year-old Clinton daughter. By the end of 1793 they were engaged and were married in the fall of the following year.

With such Republican support, Genêt became engaged in outfitting ships in American ports—to the extent that Jefferson had to request Genêt to cease such activities. Despite Jefferson's request, Genêt took it upon himself to continue this practice and at the same time telling Jefferson that France had the right to do so. Genêt went on to explain to a Pennsylvania Republican that he repudiated America's neutrality because the authority for which lay with Congress, not the president.

This intrusion into American government operations precipitated a debate on which branch was authorized to establish a neutrality policy. To inform the public about the Neutrality Proclamation, Hamilton again resorted to the press—this time the *Gazette of the United States.* In a series of articles he stressed the idea, among other reasons, that it was the duty of the president to preserve the peace until a war might be declared.

Both Jefferson and Madison expressed their belief that foreign policy was in the province of Congress except when the Constitution granted the president specific powers. They also insinuated that in this instance the neutrality proclamation was tied in with leanings to Great Britain. When Washington was advised of these innuendos by a member of the State Department, he called for a cabinet meeting to resolve the dispute. There it was decided that the United States as a neutral nation could not allow the use of its ports for any foreign military activity. This led to the cessation of Genêt's intervention and the French government being asked for his removal. However, when the political situation in France became so gruesome under Robespierre, Hamilton persuaded the president to allow Genêt to remain in this country to avoid a certain death.

After Genêt was granted asylum he moved to upper New York State where the Genêts had two children, one named George Clinton. Cornelia died in 1810 in her thirties. Genêt had become an American citizen and married again.

CLINTON PREPARES FOR POSSIBLE WAR WITH GREAT BRITAIN

Although Clinton had supported all along Washington's neutrality policy for reasons already noted, he was more supportive than ever with the growing concern that New York was woefully unprepared in the event of war. Accordingly, in January 1794 Clinton asked the legislature for funds to fortify New York City and the western frontier. This request

12. Edmond Charles Genêt (1763–1834). Painting by Ezra Ames (1768–1836) ca. 1810, oil on wood panel. Albany Institute of History and Art, bequest of George Clinton Genêt (1909.21). Cornelia Clinton Genêt. Emmet Collection, Miriam and Ira D. Wallach Division of Art, Prints, and Photographs, New York Public Library, Astor, Lenox, and Tilden Foundations. Used with permission.

was turned down by the Federalist-controlled assembly because it could be a provocative signal to Great Britain. But, just a little than two months later, in the second week of March, Clinton's misgivings of what could happen came about when it was learned that the British had seized nearly 300 American ships and held them captive in the Caribbean. This belligerent action prompted Hamilton to recommend raising taxes to pay for a military build-up. The legislature responded with an appropriation of $75,000. Then, after reports of skirmishes on the frontier, another fund was voted to repair forts in the west as well as on Governors Island off New York City.

PLANS TO RETIRE FROM OFFICE

The threat of war soon led to Republicans regaining legislative seats. However, this trend began to lessen with Clinton's announcement in January 1795 of his intentions to retire. Clinton had been in ill health for some time and his fatigued condition persisted on into 1797. Spaulding notes that during this time Washington wrote several letters of best wishes and invited Clinton to visit him in Mount Vernon when once well again.[9] During Clinton's convalescence, Justice Jay, then serving as a special diplomatic envoy to Great Britain, ran for governor and soundly defeated Robert Yates the Republican candidate.

Clinton was fifty-six when he was succeeded as governor after having served 30 years in public office. In what proved to be a five-year retirement, Clinton was mostly occupied with his real estate business of buying and managing his properties. Although he could never acquire the vast amount of land possessed by some of the Dutch settlers, Clinton believed he

was doing a social service through his invest-
ments by making settlements available for the
ordinary people. On the other end of this real
estate spectrum was the transaction of historical note, culled by Kaminski, of Clinton sell-
ing half of his Greenwich Village estate to John
Jacob Astor for $75,000—a considerable sum
of money at that time.[10]

Clinton's retirement was cut short by an
appeal from Burr to help win electoral votes in
New York City for the forthcoming presidential
election—votes necessary to elect Jefferson. To
accomplish this goal, Burr had devised a plan
of forming a ticket receptive to voters in the city
with its usual Federalist majority. Burr's ticket
would consist of war hero Horatio Gates, well-
known Judge Livingston, and Clinton. After
numerous excuses, Clinton finally consented
to run after recognizing it was his duty in helping to defeat Federalist John Adams's bid for a
second term as president.

Once the election was held and the ticket
victorious, the hunt for a vice presidential candidate began. Republican leaders chose Albert
Gallatin, then a well-known figure in Congress
and later a successor to Hamilton as secretary of
the treasury, to select the best vote-getting candidate. New York State was considered as having the best candidates in the persons of Burr
and Clinton. When the decision was reached
to name Clinton, Burr was so outraged that the
decision was reversed in his favor for the good
of the party. Clinton was just as happy with the
turn of events according to Kaminski because
Clinton believed that Burr was "the most Suitable person & perhaps the only Man" for the
job. Clinton was, in fact, "happy in having thus
got rid of the Business."[11]

7

New Leadership Within
the Republican Party

A MAJOR CHANGE IN
NEW YORK POLITICS

During Clinton's retirement the political pendulum had swung by 1800 to Republicanism, mainly on fears of problems with Great Britain. Nationwide, it seemed that Jefferson would become president with Burr as vice president.

Also during this period New York underwent a new political structure. Namely, this was the ascendancy of De Witt Clinton, George's nephew, to become head of the state's Republican party and a new means of exercising political control.

De Witt, born March 2, 1769, in New Britain, was the son of Brig. Gen. James Clinton. After graduating from Columbia and then studying law he served as secretary to Gov. Clinton. At age twenty-eight he was elected to the state senate and served until 1811. As a member of the Council of Appointments he managed to replace Federalists in many important offices and rewarded Republicans with positions according to their political abilities—thus, he became known as the originator of the "spoils system."

By the time of his uncle George Clinton's death in 1812, De Witt served as a U.S. senator, mayor of New York City, and the state's lieutenant governor, and he had proposed the building of the Erie Canal. He was elected governor for two terms: 1817–23.

GEORGE CLINTON RELUCTANTLY
ACCEDES TO ANOTHER TERM
AS GOVERNOR

In the upcoming state election of 1801 Burr was expected to run for governor but his nomination to run for the presidency removed him from consideration. Then, when Clinton turned down overtures for him to run, Chief Justice John Lansing was considered as the best candidate. However, when it appeared that a stronger candidate was necessary to be elected, a caucus of Republican leaders approached Clinton about being the candidate on the condition that he could resign the office at any time he felt unable to serve. Clinton hesitated to answer this proposal until it was learned that Burr lost out to Jefferson for the presidency— and that under the circumstances Burr might consider running for governor to retain his political posture. Kaminski suggests that De Witt was able to thwart this possibility by convincing his uncle to run for the office.[1]

Clinton's Federalist opponent was Stephen Van Rensselaer, the incumbent lieutenant governor and Philip Schuyler's son-in-law. As usual, the campaign took on airing the

PAINTED BY TRUMBULL. PUBLISHED BY JOSEPH DELAPLAINE S.W. CORNER OF CHESNUT & 7TH PHILADA ENGRAVED BY LENEY.
1813

DE WITT CLINTON ESQR

13. De Witt Clinton, Esq. Engraving by William Satchwell Leney following a painting by John Trumbull, 1813. Collection of The New-York Historical Society. Used with permission.

differences in party philosophy. While the Republicans were claiming that the Federalists were still beholden to unequal privileges inherited from England, the Federalists resurrected their citing of Clinton's criticism of the Constitution and his party's liberal ties. And, while Van Renssalaer, around forty years old, was described as too young and inexperienced for the job, Clinton was being criticized for being the richest man in the nation through his land dealings. In the midst of the campaign Burr found it prudent to openly oppose Van Renssalaer, causing Hamilton to chastise Burr, as the vice president, for meddling in a state campaign.

When the election votes were counted, Clinton had won by a big majority, including a Republican victory in Manhattan for the first time. The carrying of the city vote marked a turning point in state politics.

No sooner were the election results known than Burr became the target for his aggressiveness in building his political power base at both the national and state levels. Apropos of these dealings Jefferson came to the point of asking Clinton to forestall some of Burr's federal appointments. On the state level De Witt Clinton, in exercising his Council of Appointment powers, did such far-reaching replacement of positions once held by Federalists that the governor became most critical of his nephew's "sweeping the house." In contrast and in a showing of equanimity, the governor succeeded in having appointments made to a number of those recommended by Burr. Nevertheless, as Kaminski points out, the Clintons remained close to each other despite such differences.[2]

AGAIN, THE GOVERNOR IS CONSUMED WITH FINANCIAL MATTERS

Clinton in his seventh term as governor met with modest success in having the legislature allocate funds for enlarging the militia and for additional fortifications around New York City. Through implementation of his fiscal policies Clinton before the end of his term witnessed the end of residency taxes while road and waterways were being improved.

But it was the perennial problem with banks that remained the governor's bugaboo. In a change of heart Clinton had accepted the proposal for a bank of the United States as a place for New York to invest its surplus funds as opposed to their being placed with Hamilton's Bank of New York, which had been formed without a state charter in 1784. At the same time Clinton was also concerned that the Manhattan Bank established by Burr and his associates could make loans on favorable terms to the wealthy and to those with political connections to the exclusion of others who needed financial assistance. During 1803 a proposal

for another bank in New York City initiated by Hamilton was turned down by the Assembly as being unnecessary. The situation would continue until groups of small businessmen started obtaining charters for state banks.

AN ENTANGLEMENT IN FOREIGN AFFAIRS

The Treaty of 1783 with Great Britain had given United States navigation rights on the Mississippi and the right to use the port of New Orleans. Spain, by not being a party to the treaty, disallowed this right until 1794 when permission was granted as part of the Pinckney Treaty with the United States. Then, in 1802, Spain, involved with behind-the-scene dealings with other countries, announced its intention to prohibit use of the port. With more than 250 American ships using New Orleans for exporting goods the prospects of losing this lucrative trade led Jefferson, as president, to seek the support of state legislatures to provide additional backing to cope with whatever situation that could develop. After Maryland had made a formal complaint, Clinton recommended similar action to the New York legislature. Instead, the legislature produced a statement expressing the belief that this was in the province of the president to resolve the matter on his own. Fortunately, no further action was necessary because Spain and France, who at that time were in a war with Great Britain, had secretly agreed for Spain to transfer all of the Louisiana Territory to France then governed by Napoleon.

Recognizing that this development was a threat to American territorial interests, Jefferson arranged for an envoy to plant the idea into Napoleon's thinking that French ownership could lead to an alliance between the United States and Great Britain. Whatever influence this may have had, it was the need for money to conduct his European wars that

DEATH OF ALEX. HAMILTON.

14. The Hamilton-Burr duel. Courtesy of the New York Public Library, Astor, Lenox and Tilden Foundations.

drove Napoleon to arrange for France to sell the Louisiana Territory to the United States for $15 million.

CLINTON'S PLAN TO RETIRE CAUSES A POLITICAL DILEMMA

Once again Clinton had come to the point of advising his nephew and a few trusted friends that he would decline another term of governor if nominated. De Witt was against any such development because he was sure Burr would run for the office and if elected Burr would erode De Witt's control of the state's Republicans. He was so concerned about this prospect that he went to Jefferson for his help in convincing George Clinton to run. However, Jefferson as president felt that he had to deny this request.

Meanwhile, matters became more tenuous for De Witt on learning that Burr was seeking the support of Federalists to succeed his uncle. This in turn caused Hamilton to try to dissuade such support. When failing in this effort Hamilton decided to endorse the newly nominated moderate Republican candidate, Chancellor John Lansing, who eventually gave way to Chief Justice Morgan Lewis as the party's candidate. The ensuing election was a major victory for the Republican party.

It was within two months that the embittered Burr challenged Hamilton to a duel. Hamilton's death together with Burr's election defeat would change the political situation in New York and in the nation.

8

Clinton Becomes Vice President

CLINTON ELECTED UNDER NEW VOTING PROCEDURES

Because of the problem caused by a vice president being elected by coming in second in the electoral voting, Congress in 1804 enacted the 12th Amendment to the Constitution, which provides that the electors vote separately for a president and vice president. Jefferson and Clinton were the first to be elected under this new procedure. It was none other than Burr, as vice president, who had the duty of opening the sealed envelope containing the ballots and learning that Clinton had defeated John Breckinridge of Kentucky by 67 to 20 votes. The Republicans carried all of the states with the exception of Connecticut, Delaware, and Maryland.

The Senate over which Clinton would preside, as described by Spaulding, was a small chamber accommodating the 34 senators representing the 17 states at that time. Spaulding went on to explain that the Senate did not have the prestige nor the more distinguished membership composing the larger House of Representatives.[1]

It was in this confined setting that Clinton soon missed the active leadership he had exercised as governor for so many years. Moreover, during his term the Senate was not involved in matters of unusual importance that would require Clinton's consuming attention. This

lack of enthusiasm was in sharp contrast to the conduct of his predecessor Aaron Burr who had served in a term with more debatable issues. Burr took advantage of the close confines of the assemblage to expound at length on his ideas.

Under these circumstances Clinton spent as much time as possible in visiting his family in Poughkeepsie and then would have one his daughters accompany him by carriage or coach back to the capital. In Washington, where he preferred to reside in a boarding house, it was also to his liking not to enter into the social activities enjoyed by many of his associates.

A CHANGING SCENE IN NEW YORK WHILE CLINTON WAS IN WASHINGTON

The Clinton-Livingston coalition that had elected Justice Lewis as governor started to come apart when Lewis became embattled with De Witt Clinton's patronage appointments. Being caught in the middle of this struggle the more conservative Livingston contingent decided to join the Federalists, who went on to win the 1806 legislative election. Some Republican leaders were so alarmed with the election results that they considered teaming up with Burr to right the ship—with De Witt Clinton as one of the secret instigators. But most Clinton Republicans objected to such an alliance, and when George Clinton got wind of the possibility

15. George Clinton as vice president, 1814. Painting by Ezra Ames, oil on canvas, 53 x 41 in. Collection of The New-York Historical Society. Used with permission.

he warned his nephew that such a union with "Burrites" could not be trusted.

The perennial problem involving Burr came to an abrupt end when it was learned that he was part of a conspiracy. Spain and the United States were involved in a boundary dispute. Burr and Gen. James Wilkinson, illegally in the pay of Spain, had planned with the secession of several western states to invade Mexico and set up an empire with New Orleans as its capital. When this planned conspiracy became known Burr was tried but was acquitted because a treasonable act had not by then been committed. Not one to give up, Burr then went to Europe and tried unsuccessfully to enlist Napoleon's aid to conquer Florida. Thereafter, he practiced law in New York until his death in 1836.

With Burr removed from the political scene in New York, De Witt Clinton was in position to bring Burrites and other factions back into the fold of a more unified party. These efforts succeeded in the nomination of Judge Daniel Tompkins of the state supreme court to run for governor. Tompkins's defeat of the incumbent Lewis brought the Clintonians back in control.

A BREAKDOWN OF THE NEW YORK–VIRGINIA POLITICAL ALLIANCE

The Republicans having regained control of New York politics as engineered by De Witt Clinton was eyed by Jefferson as a threat to Virginia's ability to maintain its leadership of the national party. This threat was particularly serious to Jefferson who had witnessed the unusual rapid climb of the young Clinton as a leading figure in his state senate and then mayor of New York City.

In an effort to break up the Clinton uncle-nephew control of New York, Jefferson offered the governorship of the new Mississippi Territory to De Witt, who quickly turned down the

post. According to Evan Cornog in *The Birth of Empire . . . De Witt Clinton and the American Experience 1769–1828,*

> Jefferson was no doubt following the Virginia practice of seeking to neutralize the most powerful Republican in New York State, something that had earlier been accomplished by placing Burr and George Clinton in the impotent office of vice president. Jefferson doubtless wanted to maintain cordial relations with the Clintons. But at the same time, he did not wish to see De Witt Clinton and his uncle grow more powerful than they already were.[2]

Cornog went on to explain Jefferson's additional rivalry concerns caused by New York's economic growth and by having the nation's leading seaport.

THREATS OF WAR AND THE EMBARGO OF 1807

Notwithstanding sectional rivalry, the nation faced the problem of dealing with British and French violations of America's naval rights as had been encountered previously. In trying to maintain a policy of neutrality, Jefferson in 1807 decided to place an embargo on goods with the objective of causing Britain to honor American naval rights. This policy, nevertheless, placed a serious financial burden on northern commercial states. At the same time the administration was doing little to strengthen coastal and frontier defenses.

By early 1809 Vice President Clinton became convinced that war was inevitable unless a substantial armament program was undertaken. Clinton was perturbed that as vice president he had not been consulted by Jefferson on these and other matters such as political appointments. Perhaps some of this could be attributed to the burdens of the highest office. Kaminski, in *The Quotable Jefferson,* published by Princeton University Press in 2006, observes that the president's second term was "nearly as dismal as his first had been triumphal. . . . In many ways, the last year of Jefferson's presidency was rudderless as the nation drifted between war and peace."[3]

RIVALRY AMONG VIRGINIA'S REPUBLICANS

The rivalry had a strange way of manifesting itself in some respects with John Randolph, a Virginia Republican leader, and his followers opposing the embargo because in their opinion its enactment was outside the province of the president. These men were also opposed to Jefferson's policies of expanding the role of executive branch, such as his involvement in the Louisiana Purchase and his support of the Bank of the United States, which they cited as usurping congressional power. These deep-seated convictions led to their searching for political allies with the same persuasions.

A serendipitous boon in this search came with James Monroe joining the Randolph group. In this case Monroe was at odds with Secretary of State Madison who objected to the draft of a treaty Monroe had negotiated with Great Britain before the embargo.

As noted earlier, Madison had composed a third of the Federalist Papers in support of passage of the Constitution. Madison, nevertheless, held to the conviction that the powers of the federal government were restricted to those specifically granted by the Constitution. This philosophy led to a political relationship with Jefferson who later on appointed Madison as his secretary of state, an office he held until he became president.

Monroe studied law under Jefferson after participating in the Revolution. This was followed by a term as a U.S. senator and two terms as governor. In 1803 Jefferson appointed him to diplomatic missions regarding Louisiana

and Great Britain—the latter concerning the impressing of American seamen. Monroe was elected governor of Virginia once again and resigned to become secretary of state under Madison. He was elected president in 1816 but it was not until years later that he authored the Monroe Doctrine proclaiming no further European colonization in the new world nor further political entanglements.

THE STAGE IS SET FOR THE ONCOMING PRESIDENTIAL ELECTION OF 1808

In observing the breakdown in political alliances both outside and within Virginia, Morgan Lewis, the recently defeated governor of New York, arranged to meet with Jefferson to offer his help in backing Madison as the president's successor. This meeting may have prompted other ideas beyond the support of Madison to the extent of breaking up New York into two states thereby weakening it and ensuring, in the words in a letter from George Clinton to his nephew, "Virginia's perpetual dominion over the states, and perpetual succession to the Presidency."

Such possible developments in assisting Madison's candidacy led Monroe supporters to advocate his aligning with Clinton—with the idea of the elder Clinton as the presidential candidate and Monroe as his running mate. This arrangement had the backing of Republican leaders in both New York and Virginia.

Those promoting Madison were in a search for a running mate. In this pursuit Sen. Stephen Rowe Bradley of Vermont, president of the 1804 congressional caucus, invited all Republican members of Congress to meet and choose the candidate. Around 50 senators did not attend because they believed the invitation was an usurpation of power. After Sen. Bradley removed himself from chairing the meeting, 83 of the remaining members voted to nominate Madison for the presidency. But, at the

16. James Madison, engraving after a painting by Gilbert Stuart. Courtesy of the Library of Congress. James Monroe, from a portrait by Rembrandt Peale. Courtesy of the James Monroe Museum and Memorial Library, Fredericksburg, Virginia.

same time Clinton received 79 out of 88 votes for a second term as vice president.

Clinton supporters did not accept the caucus's action, and Clinton himself believed he was due the presidential nomination. Clinton, nevertheless, did not voice his reactions because he did not believe in "politicking" while in office. This stand, however, took on a different attitude by February 1808 when Clinton became convinced that war was inevitable unless necessary military defenses could immediately be constructed.

THE CAMPAIGN BEGINS TO HEAT UP

With the imminent threat of war looming, Clinton realized his remaining silence could be a disaster to the nation if Madison's election would be a continuance of Jefferson's policy.

Thus, Clinton realized the necessity of speaking out on important issues by becoming an active candidate.

Also refusing to accept the results of the Bradley caucus was Randolph who had succeeded in enlisting Monroe as Clinton's running mate—the strategy being, that with Clinton's popularity in the northern states, the smaller Virginia contingent would have a better chance of defeating Madison. Prospects for this ticket were heightened with the governors of Pennsylvania and Massachusetts offering their support.

Meanwhile, the Federalists were seeking an opportunity to dislodge the Jefferson and Virginia oriented Republican party. In August 1808 about 25 well-known party members met secretly in New York City in what Kaminski states was known as the nation's first nominating convention.[4] Although realizing the greater impact of a Clinton-Monroe ticket it was decided to nominate Federalists Charles Pinckney and Rufus King.

With Clinton serving as vice president it was his backers who launched a vigorous newspaper and pamphlet campaign throughout the country. In Pennsylvania the *Democratic Press* and the *Aurora* denounced the Bradley caucus and came out in support of Clinton. At the same time these newspapers were opposed to Madison for his "association" with the Sedition Act, which opposed freedom of the press and contained other restrictive measures later overturned. Madison was also disliked for his part in engineering the move of the capital to Virginia. Clinton, on the other hand, while his candidacy was being questioned around the country because of his advanced years (age sixty-nine), was acclaimed by others for his additional years of experience and being in the natural position to move into the presidency.

FAILURE TO BE ELECTED PRESIDENT OF THE UNITED STATES

As the campaign began to wind down a serious erosion set in for Clinton in New York with Chancellor Livingston, the Lewis and Burr followers opting for Madison—with Livingston endorsing Jefferson's appeasement policy. The net result was the legislature giving Madison 13 electoral votes to 6 for Clinton.

In Pennsylvania the situation became even worse for Clinton. The Republican committee upon concluding that Clinton could only win with Federalist support decided to forego Clinton and cast all 20 electoral votes for Madison.

In Virginia the electors cast all of their votes for Madison and then all for Clinton as vice president but only as a means of giving greater appeal to the ticket. When all the electoral votes were counted the tally was: Madison 122 to Pinckney's 47 for president. For vice president it was Clinton 113 to King's 47, with John Langdon of New Hampshire, Madison, and Monroe each receiving 3 votes.

CLINTON MANAGES TO SERVE MOST OF HIS TERM DESPITE POOR HEALTH

Those concerned about Clinton's age were vindicated when ill health set in, particularly after the death of his daughter Cornelia in 1810, which was a great loss to him.

Even with deteriorating health Clinton came to the fore on important issues when he could. One such case was mustering support necessary to pass a bill in 1809 for enlarging the navy, which Clinton had advocated for so long. And then it was the problems involving the Bank of the United States that Clinton wanted to have resolved.

During the 20 years of the bank's operations there had been a noticeable growth of state banks reducing the need for many functions performed by the central, federal bank. Then, too, there had been a growing opposition to the bank because of the belief that its stock was widely held in England. Other opposition stemmed from the dislike by many of Secretary of Treasury Albert Gallatin, who was an ardent champion of the bank.

When the renewal of the charter came up for a vote in the House of Representatives the preponderate number of Republicans were able to defeat its renewal.[5] In the Senate the rechartering took on a vigorous battle for votes. In the end 7 Federalists and 10 Republicans voted to recharter while 17 other Republicans, under Henry Clay's leadership, voted against a recharter. This tie vote enabled Clinton to cast the vote in removing the Bank of the United States from the financial scene.

While defeat of the bank brought on the wrath of Madison and his cohorts, it was welcomed by Republicans, including the young Martin Van Buren who was making a rise in

New York politics and would go on to become the nation's eighth president in 1837. Also welcoming the demise of the bank was De Witt Clinton who would be elected governor and who, according to Spaulding, was considered the most likely anti-Madison candidate for the presidency in the next election.[6]

∾

IN THE EARLY SPRING of 1812 Clinton's health began to fail seriously and he became stricken with pneumonia. The end came for him on April 20.

Clinton was accorded the highest honors in both his home state and in the nation. He was buried in the Congressional Cemetery on the east side of Washington. In commenting on the burial the *National Intelligencer* wrote that it was "in the presence of more people than had ever before assembled in the capital city."[7]

Later, in 1908, his body was moved to Old Dutch Church cemetery in Kingston, New York.

Notes

PREFACE

1. Kaminski is the founder and director of the Center for the Study of the American Constitution at the University of Wisconsin-Madison and is the author of other related books and treatises.

2. Kaminski's writings were invaluable in dealing with Clinton's involvement in the interpretation of the Constitution during his vice presidencies.

3. Lincoln Diamant, *Chaining the Hudson: The Fight for the River in The American Revolution* (New York: Fordham Univ. Press, 2004), xiii. Diamant quotes Washington's letter and also discusses construction of obstacles to impede ship movement on the Hudson River.

4. Joseph J. Ellis, *His Excellency George Washington* (New York: Alfred A. Knopf, 2004) 157.

1. LEADING UP TO A POLITICAL LIFE

1. John P. Kaminski, *George Clinton: Yeoman Politician of the New Republic* (Madison: Madison House Publishers, Inc., 1993) 11. Kaminski details the Clinton family background and George Clinton's forebear's move to America.

2. Kaminski, *Yeoman Politician*, 12.

3. E. Wilder Spaulding, *His Excellency George Clinton: Critic of the Constitution* (Norwood, Mass: Ira J. Friedman, Inc./The Macmillan Co., 1964) 12-17. Spaulding gives a vivid account of Clinton's experience during his service on the *Defiance*.

4. Kaminski, *Yeoman Politician*, 4.

5. Kaminski, *Yeoman Politician*, 16. Kaminski discusses effects of the Mc Dougall affair.

6. Spaulding, 30, 32, 267. Spaulding describes Clinton's family situation.

7. Kaminski, *Yeoman Politician*, 17.

8. Spaulding, 267.

9. Spaulding, 38. In a footnote he attributes the quotation about Clinton not drawing his sword against the King to Thomas Jones, *History of New York during the Revolutionary War* (2 vols., New York, 1879), II, 328.

10. Spaulding, 49. Clinton's absence from the signing the Declaration of Independence is explained by Spaulding on page 49.

2. CLINTON AS WARTIME GOVERNOR

1. Because a considerable amount of the text is concerned with the Revolutionary War, I found it expedient to use the statistics of the Americans killed, injured and captured in battle as those presented in *The Concise Illustrated History of the American Revolution* published by The National Historical Society in 1972.

2. In giving the sources of quotations and observations, an exception is made regarding correspondence wherein the text makes clear the people, situations, and time references involved.

3. Diamont, 20. Beginning on page 20 of *Chaining the Hudson*, Diamont gives an account of the invention and memorable exploits of the world's first submarine.

4. Diamont, 31.

5. David McCullough, *1776* (New York: Simon & Schuster, 2005) 231. McCullough states that based on the minutes of the council of war meeting George Clinton was the only general opposed to the withdrawal from New York City. Spaulding, however, states that General Heath was also in opposition. Spaulding, 62.

6. Spaulding 63. Spaulding's quotation about the continental army being inspired after the Battle of Harlem Heights is on page 63.

7. McCullough, 234. McCullough's observation about the battle at White Plains is given on page 234.

8. Spaulding, 83. Spaulding's statement regarding the sacking of Kingston by the British appears on page 83.

9. Spaulding, 90. The observation about General Scott as an unlikely candidate for the governorship election is stated by Spaulding on page 90.

10. James B. Bell, *The Imperial Origins of the King's Church in Early America, 1607–1783* (Basingstoke, UK: Palgrave Macmillan, 2004), 164-65, 187-202. The ending of relations between Anglican churches in America and the Church of England is dealt with in depth.

3. THE WAR EXPANDS TO THE WEST

1. *Sullivan Clinton Campaign, 1779: In Pennsylvania and New York* (Chemung Co. Historical Society, 1979). Excerpts from Alexander Fleck's address were taken from the introduction to this booklet published in 1979 by "A group of County Historians from 12 counties."

2. *Sullivan Clinton Campaign* pamphlet, 12. The historians present an unflattering assessment of General Sullivan.

3. Kaminski, *Yeoman Politician*, 63. New York's claim to the Vermont territory goes back to the ruling of the "king in Council" as discussed by Kaminski.

4. Kaminski, *Yeoman Politician*, 64. Kaminski discusses Clinton's beliefs concerning Vermont.

4. NEW YORK AFTER CORNWALLIS'S SURRENDER

1. Spaulding, 158. Spaulding discusses Clinton at the height of his career.

2. John P. Kaminski, Conference Papers, "George Clinton in Retrospect," *The Governor and the Commander in Chief: A Study in Admiration and Friendship,* September 1989. Kaminski describes the three-week trip to the Mohawk area at the George Clinton Conference on September 12, 1989 in Kingston, New York.

5. FORMING THE FEDERAL GOVERNMENT

1. Spaulding, 167. Spaulding presents a summary of the reasons for specifying state rights in the new Constitution.

2. Kaminski, *Yeoman Politician,* 130.

3. Kaminski, *Yeoman Politician,* 131.

6. INVOLVEMENT IN NATIONAL AFFAIRS

1. Kaminski, *Yeoman Politician,* 170. Kaminski presents his observations concerning the far-reaching importance in the selection of the first vice president.

2. Editorial, Philadelphia *Federal Gazette.* Dec. 13, 1788.

3. Ron Chernow, *Alexander Hamilton* (New York: Penguin Press, 2004) 273-74. Chernow describes Hamilton's envy of Clinton's popularity and his unsavory remarks against Clinton.

4. Chernow, 274.

5. A Citizen, *New York Journal.* September 1789.

6. Kaminski, *Yeoman Politician,* 232. Kaminski provides Hamilton's assessment of Clinton's and Burr's characters and experience.

7. Kaminski, *Yeoman Politician,* 233. Another observation of far-reaching importance is Kaminski's judgment concerning the birth of the Republican party.

8. Chernow, 440. Chernow presents the neutrality matter.

9. Spaulding, 218. Spaulding tells of Washington's correspondence with Clinton.

10. Kaminski, *Yeoman Politician,* 250. During Clinton's short-lived retirement he was involved in the sale of his properties, including the one to Astor, toward establishing an estate for his children.

11. Kaminski, *Yeoman Politician,* 25, 249. Kaminski discusses Clinton's about-face feelings toward Burr.

7. NEW LEADERSHIP WITHIN THE REPUBLICAN PARTY

1. Kaminski, *Yeoman Politician,* 271.

2. Kaminski, *Yeoman Politician,* 262. Clinton continued to have a close personal relationship with his nephew despite De Witt's excesses with his "Spoils System."

8. CLINTON BECOMES VICE PRESIDENT

1. Spaulding, 279, 280. Clinton's time in Washington as vice president was far from pleasant.

2. Evan Cornog, *The Birth of Empire: De Witt Clinton and the American Experience, 1769-1828* (New York: Oxford Univ. Press, 1998) 84. Cornog gives a run-down of Jefferson's concerns about New York's strong political relationships and its economic growth which combined could overtake Virginia as the power base of the Republican party.

3. John P. Kaminski, *The Quotable Jefferson* (Princeton: Princeton Univ. Press, 2006) liv, lv. Kaminski discusses Jefferson's problems of decision making after becoming president for the second time.

4. Kaminski, *Yeoman Politician,* 262. Kaminski describes the first meeting of a nominating committee.

5. Charles Chauncey Binney, *The Life of Horace Binney with Selections from His Letters* (Philadelphia: J.B. Lippincott Company, 1903), 64-65. Politics were involved in the vote on rechartering the bank as Horace Binney, one of the directors of the Bank, went to Washington in the winter of 1811 in an effort to aid the cause of renewal. In looking back on his excursion, Binney was under the impression "that the policy of the administration was to get a renewal, if they could do it without too much responsibility, and if they could not, to throw the responsibility of refusing it on George Clinton, who was Vice President, and was feared as a future opponent of Mr. Madison."

6. Spaulding, 301. Spaulding further stated that Van Buren believed a large majority of the people approved of Clinton's vote to end the charter which also enhanced De Witt's prospects against Madison.

7. Washington *National Intelligencer*, April 21, 1812.

Bibliography

Alexander, Holmes. *Aaron Burr: The Proud Pretender.* Harper and Brothers, 1937.

Appleby, Joyce. *Inheriting The Revolution: The First Generation of Americans.* Belknap Press/Harvard Univ. Press, 2000.

———. *Thomas Jefferson.* Time Books, 2003.

Banning, Lance. *The Sacred Fire of Liberty: James Madison and the Founding of the Federal Republic.* Cornell Univ. Press, 1995.

Bell, James B. *The Imperial Origins of the King's Church in Early America, 1607–1783.* Palgrave Macmillan, 2004.

Berkin, Carol. *A Brilliant Solution: Inventing the American Constitution.* Harcourt, 2002.

Biddle, Charles. *Autobiography of Charles Biddle.* E. Clayton and Co., 1883.

Brockhiser, Richard. *Alexander Hamilton.* American Free Press, 1999.

Chernow, Ron. *Alexander Hamilton.* Penguin Press, 2004.

Cornog, Evan. *The Birth Of Empire: De Witt Clinton and the American Experience, 1769–1828.* Oxford Univ. Press, 1998.

The Concise Illustrated History of the American Revolution. National Historical Society, 1972.

Cooke, Jacob Ernest. *Alexander Hamilton.* Charles Scribner's Sons, 1982.

Cresson, W. P. *James Monroe.* Univ. of North Carolina Press, 1946.

Diamant, Lincoln. *Chaining the Hudson: The Fight for the River in the American Revolution.* Fordham Univ. Press, 2004.

Ellis, Joseph J. *His Excellency George Washington.* Alfred A. Knopf, 2004.

Fleming, Thomas. *Duel: Alexander Hamilton, Aaron Burr and the Future of America.* Basic Books, 1999.

Kaminski, John P. *George Clinton: Yeoman Politician of the New Republic.* Madison House Publishers, 1993.

———. *The Governor and the Commander in Chief: A Study in Admiration and Friendship.* Conference papers, "George Clinton in Retrospect," Sept. 1989, Kingston, N.Y.

———. *The Quotable Jefferson.* Princeton Univ. Press, 2006.

Labunski, Richard. *James Madison and the Struggle for the Bill Of Rights.* Oxford Univ. Press, 2006.

McCullough, David. *1776.* Simon and Schuster, 2005.

———. *John Adams.* Simon and Schuster, 2001.

McDowell, Bart. *The Revolutionary War.* National Geographic Society, 1967.

New York Journal, September 1789.

Peterson, Merrill D., ed. *James Madison: A Biography in His Own Words.* Newsweek, 1974.

Philadelphia Federal Gazette. Dec. 13, 1788.

Schecter, Barnet. *The Battle for New York: The City at the Heart of the American Revolution.* Walker and Co., 2002.

Smith, James Morton, ed. *The Republic of Letters: The Correspondence Between Thomas Jefferson and James Madison, 1776–1826.* W. W. Norton and Co., 1995.

Sosin, Jack M. *The Revolutionary Frontier.* Holt, Rinehart and Winston, 1967.

Spaulding, E. Wilder. *His Excellency George Clinton: Critic of the Constitution.* Ira J. Friedman, Inc./ Macmillan Co., 1964.

Sullivan Clinton Campaign, 1779: In Pennsylvania and New York. Chemung Co. Historical Society, 1979.

Index

Italic page number denotes illustration.